RAISING KIDS WITH Sensory Processing Disorders

A Week-by-Week Guide to Solving Everyday Sensory Issues

RAISING KIDS WITH Sensory Processing Disorders

Rondalyn V. Whitney, Ph.D., OTR/L,
and Varleisha Gibbs, OTD, OTR/L

Prufrock Press Inc.
Waco, Texas

Library of Congress Cataloging-in-Publication Data

Whitney, Rondalyn Varney.
Raising kids with sensory processing disorders : a week-by-week guide to solving everyday sensory issues / by Rondalyn V. Whitney, Ph.D. & Varleisha Gibbs, OTD.
pages cm
Includes bibliographical references.
ISBN 978-1-61821-085-2 (pbk.)
1. Perceptual disorders in children. 2. Sensory integration dysfunction in children. 3. Children with perceptual disabilities--Education. 4. Developmentally disabled children--Rehabilitation. I. Gibbs, Varleisha, 1978- II. Title.
RJ496.P15W48 2013
618.928588--dc23

2013025385

Edited by Lacy Compton

Layout design by Raquel Trevino

ISBN-13: 978-1-61821-085-2

Printed in the United States of America.

Prufrock Press Inc.
P.O. Box 8813
Waco, TX 76714-8813
Phone: (800) 998-2208
Fax: (800) 240-0333
http://www.prufrock.com

Table of Contents

Activities

MORNING ROUTINES

MEALTIME ROUTINES

SCHOOL

BEDTIME ROUTINES

HOLIDAYS

SOCIAL PARTICIPATION

Acknowledgements

We are fortunate to work at the University of the Sciences and receive ongoing encouragement for our commitment to promote quality of life (QoL) for children and their families, so we must begin by expressing our gratitude to the Department of Occupational Therapy in Samson College of Health Sciences at USciences. Several students contributed to this book, sharing their ideas for activities, providing feedback, or investigating the evidence to support the activities we selected. We acknowledge Ashley Costa, Hyan Shin, Delaina Torres, and Christopher Yang for their mealtime ideas, and Kaitlin Carll, Maureen Golden, and Stephanie McAllister for their activity ideas and for their research to ensure the activities in the book were supported by the evidence of our profession. Above all, we acknowledge Alyssa Brennan, an extraordinary student who stepped forward and provided enthusiastic contribution to the manuscript's beauty, organization, and fun. Thank you, Alyssa. Dr. Gigi Smith's research on sensory-based supports and barriers to quality of life and mealtime routines was critical to inform the activities provided. We thank Sue Finkelstein for inspiring the Two Truths and a Lie activity. We are extremely grateful to those who provided scholarly peer review of the book to ensure the science was translated accurately: Dr. Paula Kramer, Dr. Gigi Smith, and Dr. Claudia Hilton.

We also need to thank our external reviewers for this book:

- Paula Kramer, Ph.D., OTR, FAOTA, Professor, Program Director for the Doctoral Program, University of the Sciences
- Claudia Hilton, Ph.D., MBA, OTR/L, FAOTA

This is a book for families, to promote family quality of life (FQoL), and we would each like to thank our extraordinary families. Rondalyn thanks Bill, her rock and husband, and her two sensational boys—sensory underresponsive Zac and sensory-craving Alex—and her own mother, Maggie, who followed her intuition to provide a sensational life of soft fabrics and calm environments for her sensory overresponsive daughter. And to Frances M., who planted the seed for the idea for a book of activities to help families with sensational children.

Varleisha would like to thank Tennessee, Dakota, and Georgie for always supporting her, allowing her the time to achieve her goals, and making her a better therapist. Also, to her mother, sister, and grandparents for always believing and teaching her strength! And, she offers deep gratitude to the faculty at the University of the Sciences occupational therapy department, for their guidance and mentorship.

Foreword

> "We do not need magic to transform our world. We carry all of the power we need inside ourselves already."—J. K. Rowling

I believe that the quote above from an interview with J. K. Rowling provides an important framework for thinking about this book, *Raising Kids With Sensory Processing Disorders*. Parenting children is a fun but difficult and complex task, even with a child without any problems. (Does such a child exist?) But when you have a child with a sensory processing disorder, parenting can sometimes seem like a monumental task. Believe me, I know—I have been a therapist for more than 35 years and I have a child with Attention Deficit Disorder and sensory processing issues. And even with the knowledge that I have, day-to-day activities at times seemed like quite a challenge! But have no fear: This book is here to help you through those challenging days.

It is amazing to observe an occupational therapist work with a child with sensory processing disorders and see a sudden change in that child. After engaging in what looks like simple activities, the child's behavior has changed. That child may become more compliant, or calmer, or more animated, or more able to interact with others. It looks like the therapist is performing some special kind of magic. But it is not magic at all. It is simply the application of a very specific knowledge of the child's sensory system.

This book can provide you with an overview of that knowledge so that you can be a very active participant in the "magical" growth of your child. You will not become therapists (or magicians), but you will have a basic understanding of what is going on with your child, and have lots of ways that you can help him or her grow, develop, and cope with the everyday challenges that he or she faces. This book is filled with basic explanations of sensory processing disorder, techniques to help you deal with day-to-day problems, and specific activities to help you through those trying days. Incorporating these activities and techniques in your daily life can make a world of difference to your child.

Dr. Whitney and Dr. Gibbs are dear friends of mine and very accomplished therapists. They are sharing their knowledge and experience with you so that you can become an important partner in promoting growth and change in your child. The change will not happen overnight, but with continued effort and input you should see daily activities become easier and your child become more successful.

Magic will not transform your world or change your child, but the increased knowledge that this book provides will help you make that important step forward. The power that you have within you is the desire to help your child and the willingness to learn what you can do in order to assist your child to become more functional every day. Knowledge is power, and Dr. Whitney and Dr. Gibbs have given you the power to help your child move forward.

Paula Kramer, Ph.D., OTR, FAOTA
Professor of Occupational Therapy

Part I

About Sensory Processing Disorders

Chapter 1

Demystifying Sensory Processing Problems

Every family has its own unique habits, routines, and rituals that allow for organization and support engagement in daily life activities. But if you are reading this book, it's likely that your child is having some difficulty being a kid—something is in the way of allowing him to engage in the day-to-day tasks and activities in which you would expect him to engage. Maybe he can't stand hearing his brother chew spaghetti. Maybe she screams and thrashes when it's time to change out of her pajamas. Maybe he can't go to sleep at night or is overly lethargic in the mornings. Or maybe the smell of her teacher's perfume causes her to become upset. These issues are baffling, perhaps leaving you to seek the assistance of a professional. Despite the implementation of therapeutic services, or lack thereof, your relationship with your child may be compiled of a lack of understanding and disconnect. You may ask yourself, "Do I really know my child?"

Parents sometimes wonder what occupational therapists know about their child that parents do not. How do we have the "magic key"? Although that may not be completely true, occupational therapists are trained experts in viewing your child as a unique individual, incorporating the entire family unit, and providing caregiver training for a successful intervention process. However, you are the expert for your child! Yes, you are the most important expert. If you are debating that idea, we hope to change your perception. Our aim is to enhance the vision you already possess by allowing you to look through our "glasses." Better yet, you are probably on the right path. Perhaps you have approached what feels like the edge of a cliff. Well, let's bridge the gap to complete your family's path to success.

Despite wonderful advances within the field, many still question the occupational therapist's role. More specifically, who are occupational therapists and how do we use Ayres' (1972) sensory integrative approach? And how are the components of such an approach helpful in everyday life? Sensory-related problems affect the routine of the entire family (Schaaf, Toth-Cohen, Johnson, Outten, & Benevides, 2011). As occupational therapists who specialize in working with children, our work is guided by the question of "How do the problems the child is having impact his quality of life and the quality of life of his or her family?" We are interested in the child and his family's ability to fully engage in the day-to-day activities, or occupations, important to the life of that child (e.g., getting adequate rest and sleep, being able to play with friends, and having an uninterrupted dinner with the family). During evaluations, an occupational therapist's questions may sound intrusive. However, our goal is to gain the clearest picture of your child and family. We are constantly observing how children behave even during the most basic of activities. Although this appears to be a simple process, we use theoretical and scientific evidence to broker a fit between the way your child makes sense of his body and environment and his participation in play, school, home, with friends, self-care, and learning activities.

Our philosophy is constructed on the foundation that your child is not only your child, but also a friend, a sibling, and a learner. Children are constantly growing and, therefore, constantly in a state of transition. In addition, a large role they play is that of being a student. As scientists, we study the activities that promote positive habits and routines related to the occupational role of student, and therefore homework strategies and morning routines. We are frequently invited to use the body of knowledge related to sensory processing as we observe sensory barriers interfering with an individual's ability to interact with others, adapt to the environment, and perform expected tasks, such as getting dressed or eating with the family.

Although we use social and behavioral theories, knowledge of medical science is also part of the toolbox. Our training in anatomy, physiology, and neurology helps us understand development from the basic systems of the body—the brain, the muscles, and the sensory system. Our background in psychosocial theory supports our interventions to be holistic and mindful of the spirit and the social-emotional aspects of development. We use evidence to guide our practices and the fields are science driven. Sensory processing disorder (SPD) is not an accepted diagnosis, but it has become increasingly used in clinical practice to explain behaviors that are sensory based and to describe processing through the sensory pathways that is disordered and impairs participation. Even while SPD is not an accepted diagnosis, the term can provide a framework with which parents and professionals can understand a child's abilities.

In this book, our goal is to help you see what we, as experts, would see and to provide helpful suggestions that might make daily life easier. Although occupational therapists can use wonderful strategies in the clinic, carryover to the home and community environments is the ultimate goal for our interventions. We want to help you learn how to recognize the "soft signs" that suggest a child is struggling to take in information from his environment, organize that input, and use what he's learning to grow and learn and play. As a parent, you are the expert on your child, but when there is a gap between his development and his potential, what do you do? How do you prioritize what you provide for intervention? When do you worry and when do you watch and wait? We have worked with so many parents who say, "I wish I had started earlier" or "I wish I knew this information when he was younger." We have wished that too, and this book is our gift to your child and to you. We hope to partner with you through the following pages and together close the gap between parent and practitioner strategies.

Of course, our ultimate goal is to help you close the gaps between the performance and potential of your child as he grows and thrives within your family and within the larger community. Why is sensory processing so important, and why can it be so disruptive? All learning occurs through the senses and demonstration of learning though the motor system. All nerves to the brain are sensory nerves. You learn by what you see, hear, taste, smell, and feel and how you move. Difficulties with participation related to sensory processing are characterized by the inability to take in sensory information and use that information received through the senses to function smoothly in daily life. When a child is unable to react adaptively to different sensory experiences, there can be a disruption in engaging and performing in certain contexts and environments such as in the home or at school. Instead of concentrating on the required activities, she may be anxious about the unknown that may be coming. Children who experience sensory modulation difficulties may display signs of sensory seeking, sensory overresponsiveness, or sensory underresponsiveness during the course of a day. Children can seek sensation in a less than acceptable way or can retreat from sensation. Both strategies can impair family quality of life (FQoL) and interfere with a child's primary occupations: playing, learning, and being a good friend.

This book will focus on helping the sensory system take in information from the world in a functional manner. Organization of sensory information will assist families in reducing impairment and improve quality of life through normalized patterns of participation.

BACKGROUND

Our sensory motor systems play a huge role in our ability to participate in our daily lives. All of us must be able to achieve sensory modulation, sensory discrimination, and sensory-based motor adeptness. When the sensory demands of your child's environment are a misfit with their sensory preferences, it is our job to find ways to create a better fit between the child, the environment, and the activity.

Think about the times you were in the school cafeteria or lunchroom. In that setting, you can find a glut of other people's food preferences and infinite ways that peers are interacting. You can smell peanut butter alongside pizza, hear high-pitched giggles from a gaggle of small girls, and see a quiet introvert sitting off to the edge of the more animated interactions. Where would you sit? How would you feel after the 45-minute lunch break? Would you be excited and energized or ready for an aspirin? What coping skills would you use to be successful in this setting? When there is a misfit with the environment and/or the population, children cannot fully participate in the activities of that environment. For example, a child who is very sensitive to smell, sound, and touch may absolutely fear the cafeteria! The mixture of food odors, multitude of simultaneous conversations, and the occasional peer brushing against her arm may lead to sensory overload. That overload may then result in self-isolation or simply negative behavior. Some children get overwhelmed and disregulated and act out, maybe yell at their classmates, smack them, or squirt them with juice. Others withdraw—many schools have a "peanut-free zone" and this has become the default site of retreat for non-peanut allergic but sensory sensitive kids to retreat. This manifestation of behavior is frequently the result of poor interaction with a multitude of stimuli from the environment. A family dinner can feel like an overcrowded lunchroom to some children. The ultimate goal for any of us is to create balance between one's inner and outer world.

In our experience, there are five areas that are particularly problematic for children who have delays in the development of their sensory-motor system that ultimately disrupt family routines. Both our clinical experiences and the emerging body of evidence has identified that many of these issues are the result of under- or overhypersensitivity to stimulation or are caused by poor modulation skills. Although that is an oversimplification of the nervous system, it's probably worthwhile to pause and think about modulation.

Poor modulation occurs when an individual lacks strategies that provide support or balance for the sensations that feel overwhelming. For example, a child has difficulty with getting dressed in the morning because she finds the touch of a shirt or underwear to be overwhelming. This in turn interrupts family routines and rituals and causes a stress-filled morning for the whole family. However, using what we know about the nervous system, we can provide sensory input that helps the child's nervous system feel more organized, or in balance, and therefore able to participate in the morning routine of getting dressed. Imagine this scenario:

> Joey wakes up and needs to get his clothes on but he screams and refuses to take off his pajamas. Mom is in a hurry: She has an important meeting at 9 a.m. and cannot be late, but Joey is having a tantrum. The morning is off to a rough start.

Now imagine this:

> Mom says, "Joey, time to rise and shine!" and turns on the iPod—the theme song from *Star Wars* blasts in the room, Joey sits up, and he smiles. Mom says, "We need to get dressed. Let's get your body ready!" and she and Joey begin to dance to the music, pumping their arms. When Joey's arms go up, the pajamas come off and a shirt replaces the top; the same routine happens with the bottoms and socks. Once he's dressed, Mom says, "Now who's ready for a power breakfast?" Mom serves crunchy cereal with apple chunks.

This heavy work to the nervous system involved in the breakfast Joey's mom served (e.g., chewing, moving the muscles) is organizing and allows us to modulate sensation that is very alerting (e.g., changing temperatures, changing positions, changing textures on the skin). Music provides rhythm and the opportunity to match the internal sequence and timing to the external world; dancing provides strong proprioceptive input that helps to organize the nervous system and allow the individual to better meet life's challenges—in Joey's case, getting dressed. One other piece going on here that can't be overlooked—moving to music floods the body with endorphins (Seligman, 2004). Think of these interventions as a "dose," like when we take vitamin C to prepare our bodies to ward off an attacking virus; sensory strategies are used to prepare the body for good work (e.g., dressing, eating with others, sleeping). The research isn't clear about how much and how long we need sensory input, but think of your own body—how much of a challenge can you persist against before you need to take a walk, have a coffee, or wiggle?

To help us develop strategies that will reduce impairments that families may experience, we took a careful look at the literature on sensory issues. The series of activities in this book were distilled from the real world and tested to help families develop positive habits, routines, and rituals in order to further sustain engagement in important and meaningful activities. Because none of us can make too many changes at once, we've provided a strategy a week for you to try, 52 total. We know it takes about 30 days to create a new habit—we hope using one strategy a week (maybe a few times a week) will build a repertoire of new habits that stoke your child's nervous system, promote further positive habits, and support you to have greater FQoL.

Because the use of sensory strategies is a scientifically based set of interventions, we want to take a little time in the next chapter to identify some terminology that will be utilized throughout this book. The descriptions of common sensory problems shared in Chapter 2 will later be coupled to the activities in Chapters 4–9.

PROBLEM SOLVING

We all interpret what we see—some families watch a child's reactions and think the child is behaving in a way to seek attention. Sometimes parents and teachers feel a child isn't motivated. We believe children want to be good and live up to the expectations the adults have for them. When they aren't, our experience has convinced us there is an underlying barrier to that aspiration. The same is true for parents—parents want to help their child learn prosocial behaviors and they want to provide discipline rather than punishment, but sometimes they don't see what is hiding in the background that's causing their child to behave in "crazy" way. Because of our professional training, we view breakdowns in engagement, take a developmental approach, and ask questions about the sensorimotor and cognitive system. Can the child identify what she wants to do? Can she make a plan and can her muscle system take the steps that will allow her to enact that plan? For example, is she motivated to climb on a tire swing to play with friends? And if so, can she plan how to move her muscles to make that happen? And then, can she execute that plan in a timely way or are all of the children done with recess by the time your little girl gets started on her plan? Some children want to play but are overly sensitive to noise or smell. Others seek out information for their sensory motor system in inappropriate ways, licking their friends, chewing on tree bark, or stuffing their mouths during lunchtime. Although there is disagreement in the literature about sensory process and whether or not difficulties reach the threshold of a disorder, other scientists have found this way of inaccurately interpreting sensory motor information might be classified as a sensory processing disorder. Either way, problems with processing sensory input can *really* get in the way of a child's ability to play and learn and be a good friend.

Research has found that atypical sensory experiences or difficulties with processing sensory stimuli greatly affect the family's daily life. Having a child with autism, ADHD, or other disorders that result in disruptive behaviors (e.g., tantrums, oppositionality, anxiety, fighting, etc.) can create significant stress in the family. Family impairment is predicted by child behavior and family impairment predicts poor participation in life's routines, community events, and social opportunities (Freedman & Whitney, 2011; Whitney, 2012).

Participation is limited when a child has difficulty organizing sensory information to the extent that he cannot adapt to the expectations in the environment, and something common across many diagnoses. For example, about 69% of children with ADHD also struggle to organize sensations across environments and 90% or more children with autism spectrum disorders (ASD) are challenged by sensations (Ben-Sasson, Carter, & Briggs-Gowan, 2009). New research is showing sensory overresponsivity to be a precursor of anxiety (Green & Ben-Sasson, 2010), and sensory underresponsivity correlates with depression (Mazurek et al., 2013). Recent findings also have shown that when a child seeks or avoids sensation, or struggles to understand how sensory issues impact function, this creates maternal stress and family impairment at similar levels to having a child with ASD (Whitney, 2012).

What does that all mean? Well, when families cannot participate in desired activities, (e.g., grocery shopping, church, scouts, soccer, family dinners, etc.) because of their child's habits and behaviors, a downward spiral of withdrawal begins. Families increasingly withdraw from vacationing, traveling during the holidays, social outings, or family events; they are legitimately concerned about their child's response to novel sensory experiences. You may or may not be nodding your head in agreement. If you are, you have a great understanding of how sensory issues can take over your entire family! We hope to augment your routines and make things easier. If you have not experienced such challenges, this book is perhaps great timing.

It becomes crucial to develop sensory-based strategies that will help a child, and therefore the family, sustain his engagement in different activities and turn the spiral around. Schaaf and colleagues (2011) identified that morning and evening routines were especially difficult times of the day for children who have a developmental lag in the sensory-motor system. Each context presents its own issues. We will look at the child's sensory experiences as they impact the habits, routines, rituals, and quality of life (QoL) of the family within five specific environments/contexts: morning routines, school, social experiences, bedtime, and holidays.

As therapists, we collaborate with families to create habits and routines that will help normalize their day-to-day lives (Bagby, Dickie, & Baranek, 2012; Schaaf et al., 2011). As parents, we teach and create habits, routines, and rituals to and with our children and this in turn shapes our family identity. When a family develops positive habits, routines, and rituals, positive performance is the result. Developing these can be beneficial to not only the individual's performance but also to the family system.

Habits: Think of habits as the automatic behaviors that are integrated into more complex patterns that enable people to function on a day-to-day basis and that can be useful, dominating, or impoverished. Habits can support or interfere with performance in all areas.

Routines: Routines are patterns of behavior that are observable, regular, repetitive, and provide structure for daily life. Routines can be promoting, satisfying, or damaging. Think about rituals as symbolic actions with spiritual, cultural, or social meaning, which contribute to a person's identity and can reinforce values and beliefs.

(American Occupational Therapy Association, 2008)

We will be using a problem-solving approach in this book and providing you with 52 strategies to try. Each section of the book addresses one of the six most troublesome areas of family life when raising a child with a disability: morning routines, mealtime routines, bedtime routines, school issues, holidays, and social participation. Problem solving has four steps:

- ask yourself "**What** is the problem we need to solve?",
- **isolate** what you know and what you need to know,
- try a **strategy**, and
- then **evaluate** whether or not your strategy solved the right problem.

We call this the WISE approach to problem solving, inspired by the work of Pólya (1957).

Let's learn more about what sensory motor deficits might be hiding in the background of the behaviors you find to be barriers to participation for your family. Here's an example of using the WISE approach to problem solving to determine if sensory overload is contributing to a child's meltdowns.

- Step 1: **What** is the problem? What are the reasons for sensory overload?
  - Does the child feel there is too much noise, too many people, too much to look at, or too many people wanting to talk to her?

- Step 2: **Isolate** what you know and what you need to know.
  - Does your child have a meltdown in specific situations? What do you do that seems to help your child feel calmer or get her body or emotions under control? (See the Back in Control strategy in Appendix A, p. 144).

- Step 3: **Suggest** a strategy.
  - Keep a small bag of strategies with you to give your child, such as a special toy, a juice box with a straw, a bottle of ice-cold water, or an iPod with calming music.

- Step 4: **Evaluate** whether your strategy worked: Think like a scientist.
  - Sometimes you will solve one problem, maybe not the one you intended. Evaluate your strategy, redefine the problem,

and try again. Figure 1 shows a sample Evaluate Progress chart for one family's strategy. Use the blank Evaluate Progress form in Appendix A to determine if your strategies have worked.

Now that you have the WISE strategy at your disposal, let's learn a little more about the specific sensory processing issues your child may be facing and what you can do to observe and track them.

Problem Identified/ Strategy	Goal/ Start Date	Midway Checkpoint Date	How Will You Know You Have Solved the Problem?	Date Goal Met
Tantrums during homework. Tried the jumping jacks facts activity.	3/11	4/11	Will learn multiplication facts 1–9; will ask for help instead of throwing book.	6/15

Figure 1. Sample Evaluate Progress chart.

Chapter 2

Learning About the Problems Hiding in the Background

Sometimes a child's interaction with his environment and his internal ability to respond to sensory demands is delayed. This is revealed in both physiological (internal) and behavioral (observable) responses. To better explain the concepts of adaptive response to the environment (modulation), the observable response is identified as regulation. For example, if your child is not receiving enough stimulation from his environment, he may attempt to run around to self-regulate. Our friend Joey was receiving *too much* sensation, which caused him to avoid any more stimulation (like the sensation of changing clothes). Parents can't see what we see in research labs. We can use a positron emission tomography (PET) scan and observe how the body is processing sensation in the nervous system. The internal process is the physiological response of sensory modulation. What parents, teachers, and therapists *can* see is the behavioral expression of the body's central nervous system. When we can perform optimal modulation, necessary information is taken in and organized to produce suitable behavioral responses. A good illustration of this is our ability to produce a decent dinner despite our children being noisy and running around the house. Although this example may be anxiety provoking, our systems modulate to the stimuli in our environments. Sensory modulation is a complex process that typically occurs automatically. Through experience and exposure, we are able to "take in" sensory information and decode it in our brains spontaneously. Hence, we have the capacity to assemble adjustments as required for optimal performance.

However, even for us, there is sometimes a misfit between our sensory system and the environment. Anyone who has ever attended a birthday party at one of the popular indoor children's entertainment facilities can relate. Our interaction will be different in that stimulating party environment versus our everyday environments. Although we have the ability to modulate our sensory systems, responses to sensory stimuli must be enhanced or reduced. This brings us to the terms *habituation* and *sensitization.* With habituation, repeat occurrence of a stimulus results in a decrease of response. This relates back to our example of preparing dinner with our children being noisy and running around. With sensitization, the response rate is increased to a stimulus. This speaks to how you are more alert at the party facility versus in your typical environment. Could you imagine having to make dinner in that setting? It may be challenging due to you being on high alert to ensure your child's safety in a crowded and overstimulating environment. Sensitization is needed and necessary at times. Yet, the theory guides us to understand that eventually we adjust and habituation should occur (Ayres, 1972; Parham et al., 2011).

A situation in which we are not able to adapt to our environment and are always on alert can be anxiety provoking. This anxiety may manifest in behavioral responses. *Overresponsivity* and *underresponsivity* are two terms that correlate with this notion. With overresponsivity, too much information is entering our sensory systems, resulting in high arousal levels (Miller, Anzalone, Lane, Cermak, & Osten, 2007). Just imagine standing in the doorway as students run out to the playground for recess. Overresponsivity would be like the sensory system allowing too many students through the doors at once. Your child then needs to attempt to slow them down. A behavioral response is elicited. If your child has a low threshold for sensory stimuli (Dunn, 1997, 2001), she will likely overreact! Crying, screaming, and escaping or even eloping (running away) behaviors may be her attempt to block out the unwanted stimuli. Sensory overresponsivity (SOR) is being reported at high rates in children with and without primary diagnosis such as Attention Deficit Hyperactivity Disorder (ADHD) and Autism Spectrum Disorders (ASD; Miller et al., 2007).

On the other hand, sensory underresponsivity (SUR) can occur when too little stimulation is present. We can view underresponsivity as having a high threshold for sensory stimuli. With a high threshold, stimulation is not reached. Children can also shut down in the presence of too much sensory information. Imagine you have good intentions of reading this book in its entirety one weekend, and then clean your child's room first. You become so overwhelmed by the cleaning that you take a nap instead! This is a great example of shutting down. For children with ASD, sensory underresponsiveness has been shown to be associated with impaired social and communication behaviors and repetitive behaviors (Foss-Feig, Heacock, & Cascio, 2012).

In relation to self-regulation, SOR and SUR can be observed in sensory seeking and avoiding behaviors. If your child is not receiving enough sensory information, then she may seek it out and often not in socially acceptable ways. For example, if your child feels underwhelmed by sensation (SUR), she may seek sensation in ways that are not very adaptive (e.g., making weird noises, hitting her spoon on a table or on her brother, kicking the wall or the back of the chair in front of her in a movie theater). These behaviors may surface in the presence of SUR and we look for those behaviors to give us insights about the underlying sensory nervous system. If your child feels like he is getting too much sensory input, he may try to get away from that sensation; for example, he may crawl under the table at the restaurant or scream and flail when you try to rinse his hair. These behaviors may present as frequent attempts at gross motor activity (e.g., running, climbing, crashing, jumping), mouthing objects (e.g., chewing on his shirt or pencil tops), or even desiring certain sounds or smells. In addition, there may be a pleasure component, triggering a desired response and the release of endorphins into the body. If it gives us pleasure, we will go back for more. Your child may enjoy the response he gets from sensory seeking behaviors. The activities we provide must be presented strong enough and long enough to overpower that desire-seeking activity.

SENSORY DEFENSIVENESS

Does your child have extreme reactions to having messy hands, wearing certain fabrics, or eating specific foods? These overresponsive behaviors relate to sensory defensiveness. We can each experience sensory defensiveness when we feel overwhelmed by sensation and can't seem to get organized (like being at a Talking Heads concert when you have a migraine, ouch!). Sensory defensiveness is most likely a connection with the sympathetic nervous system (SNS). Within the SNS, the fight or flight responses are triggered. For some reason, the child is interpreting the stimulus as a threat, even when it is not! When our SNS is triggered, we know there is a physiological response. The natural defense mechanisms to avoid or fight against a threat result in our muscles tensing, pupil dilation to let in needed visual information, increase of auditory information through the ears, slowing of our digestive system, and increased breathing and heart rates. If your child is presented with what she interprets as a "threat" to her sensory system, she begins letting in too much information. Pupil dilation is letting in too much light, and her ears are letting in too much sound. The stimuli actually *hurt*! You may have experienced this in a movie theatre when the sounds are too loud for you but don't seem to bother others. Instead of habituating to the stimuli, your overly sensitive child may constantly be in a state of hypervigilance, anticipating these threats. Later, we will discuss how to present these stimuli in a nonthreating way to desensitize your child to non-noxious but perceived "threatening" stimuli. We need activities that will stimulate his parasympathetic nervous system (PNS) instead. The PNS helps to regulate the body, modulating heart rate, breathing, and vital functioning (Schaaf et al., 2010).

In addition to defensiveness, gravitational insecurity may ensue. Again, the information coming in is threatening and triggering the child's SNS. When required to leave the ground, such as to climb stairs or playground equipment, the child becomes insecure, meaning he sees the required action as a threat! Children who avoid such activities, specifically during critical development stages, run the risk of low muscle tone. Hence, children may not trust their abilities to safely support and maneuver their own bodies.

DISORGANIZATION IN THE SYSTEM THAT DISCRIMINATES SENSORY INPUT

This category relates to the misinterpretation of sensory information. For example, children having trouble discriminating may not be able to identify what sounds are important, how hard they are hugging others, or appropriately identify temperatures (e.g., they may identify a lukewarm bath as hot). Our sensory systems are composed of vestibular, proprioceptive, auditory, visual, tactile, gustatory (taste), and olfactory (smell) mechanisms. Difficulty in discrimination can occur within any of those systems. For instance, with proprioception, a child may produce too much force, frequently breaking pencils and crayons. Tactile discrimination is related to being able to identify where you are being touched or how hard you are being touched and identifying an object through touch (stereognosis). When this information is limited or delivered incorrectly, overall performance in home and school activities can be affected. Difficulty within vestibular discrimination can be revealed in poor postural control, balance, and equilibrium. Unlike sensory-based motor disorders, to be discussed, this may not be in relation to hypotonia (low muscle tone). Rather, the child has difficulty distinguishing her head movements in comparison to her body.

Other areas of sensory discrimination dysfunction include gustatory issues, auditory issues, and visual discrimination challenges. Gustatory issues occur when the child has difficulty identifying variations in taste and temperature of food. With auditory issues, knowing what sound to attend to, who is talking, and where it is coming from affects the child's ability to attend in class and follow multistep commands. Visual discrimination challenges may result in difficulty distinguishing shapes and objects, figure ground, and visual closures. Hence, the most common representation of visual challenges is seen in sloppy handwriting.

DELAYS IN THE SENSORY-BASED MOTOR SYSTEM

We understand there are two types of definable delays in the sensory-motor system, postural and dyspraxia. Postural correlates to challenges in balance and core stability. It is hypothesized that low or high muscle tone, identified as hypotonia and hypertonia, may affect gross motor performance. These delays can be especially challenging for parents to identify. The child may sometimes seem strong and active. However, the strength may be in compensation for actual weakness in the core areas (i.e., trunk, pelvis, abdominal areas). In the presence of a weak core, children will tense their extremities in order to support the body. Tense muscles in the arms and legs may mask actual weakness. Often, these children appear to enjoy gross motor activities, such as sports, and have difficulty remaining seated in class. Yet, they usually do not reveal the characteristics of a child with sensory modulation disorder. They are able to reach a calm and alert state, have the abilities to self-regulate, and can discriminate incoming sensory information. The challenge for these children is the result of a misfit between their body and the environment. It is easier to move around versus sitting or standing in one place for an extended amount of time. Staying in one static position requires the cooperation of an abundance of our muscles simultaneously. When we move, our muscles take turns moving in a synergistic pattern. Children with weak cores will enjoy movement activities such as karate, baseball, and running. Yet school performance may be affected, leaving teachers and parents to ponder a diagnosis of ADHD. (We noted previously that the sensory motor system *can* be presented in diagnoses such as ADHD, however, this is not always the case.) Knowledge of this category of the sensory motor system is important as it can allow you to apply the appropriate activities to support your child's needs.

PRAXIS

Have you heard of dyspraxia or praxis? Sometimes people will inaccurately use motor planning and dyspraxia as synonyms. Praxis is a tech-

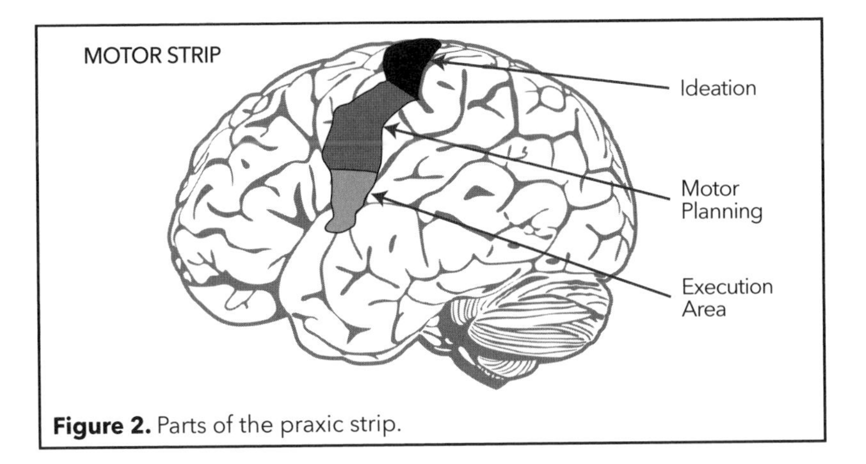

Figure 2. Parts of the praxic strip.

nical term in neurology and there are three parts in the praxic strip, corresponding to three distinct areas in the brain (see Figure 2). The first part controls ideation or having an idea of what you want to do. The second part of the praxic strip calculates how to move your muscles to act on your idea—we call this motor planning. The third part of the strip executes the plan—actually kicks you into action. Praxis is typically autonomic and necessary for everyday activities. With novel activities, we have the ability to plan and learn the new movements. When dysfunction arises, clumsiness occurs. Our central nervous system motor areas, such as the cerebellum, assist in smooth and coordinated movements. Development from conception on allows for necessary connections and pathways to be "smoothed out." When this does not occur, motor output is affected. Hence, poor sensory information is coming in, and poor movement is then produced. Premature birth, lack of exposure to certain activities (such as in sensory deprivation), and certain neurological diagnoses can affect development of our motor areas such as the cerebellum. Do not panic! In most cases, we can assist in further developing these areas by again choosing appropriate and supportive activities. Years ago, children were much more active and used their bodies more. Think of this as a dose of sensory input that developed more normal functioning. As we've migrated to a more sedentary, indoor society, many children are missing what they need for their nervous systems to develop. This book will help give you some ideas for providing a more sustained dose of activities to support optimal development.

Chapter 3

How Is Your Child "Wired"?

Are our children direct results of our parenting? Or do they have an internal blueprint that will determine their personality? This brings us to the concept of temperament. Some argue that a child's behavior is related to parenting style. Although some aspect of that may be accurate, anyone having at least two children may beg to differ. It can be quite amazing to see how different your children's personalities may be. One child may run up to new children to make friends. Your other child may grab onto your pants leg, hoping to disappear in social settings. Parents have to be aware of the innate temperament of their child as a primary component in successfully building habits and family routines.

First, let's explore your temperament. Are you an extrovert who easily engages with others socially? Or are you an introvert who prefers to stay home and read a book? Would you say you are emotional, crying easily? Perhaps it takes a lot for you to warm up to others. These are all questions you must ask yourself. Now, ask those same questions in relation to your other family members, excluding your child with sensory processing difficulties. Lastly, look at the child with sensory processing concerns and identify his temperament based on those inquiries. The following definitions will help you identify your child's temperament:

- *Introvert*: May be distant and disconnected from others; likes to unwind in private and solitude
- *Adaptable/Easygoing*: Although not extremely social, he can adjust to his environment as needed
- *Emotional*: Labile, will cry or become frustrated easily or might laugh or cry inappropriately
- *Slow to Warm*: Requires a lot to engage and get stimulated
- *Extrovert*: Easily engages with other children; craves being around others

It would be too ambitious for us to try to evaluate each member of your family in a book. However, it's important to remind you as you read along to reflect not only on your child's temperament and sensory profile, but on your profile, that of your spouse or partner, and that of the other members of your family as well. Start to think about and try to determine a "goodness of fit" between you and your child. For example, if you are a morning person (you wake up bubbly and alert and seeking sensory input) but your child is a sensory avoider (she wakes up grumpy and needs a long time to feel alert), then this is mismatch in your sensory profiles. What can you each do to modulate your sensory system so you have a better morning together? The chart in Figure 3 can offer you a thinking tool—you can produce a visual schema for you to explore, such as the graph in Figure 4. The families we have worked with have found this to be very helpful in determining areas of similarity and differences, targeted areas for creating a better fit within relationships.

The numbers within the chart correspond with how you will plot your graph. If we plotted a graph of your family's sensory profiles, it might look like the one in Figure 4. Clinically, that helps us get a picture of the areas that are interrupting FQoL. As you can see in this graph, the parents identified that the child always seeks auditory stimulation, tactile and proprioceptive input, crunchy foods, movement, and smells. The parents also identified the child as having superior motor abilities. However, there is a significant difference between the child's temperament and the parent's. Additional mismatches can be identified in a

Auditory	Visual	Tactile/ Proprioception	Crunchy Food	Mushy Food	Smells	Sensory Behavior	Temperament	Anxiety	Motor Performance
Always Avoids (10)	Always Avoids (10)	Always Avoids (10)	Always Avoids (10)	Always Avoids (10)	Always Avoids (10)	Always Avoids (10)	Introvert (10)	Frequently (10)	Clumsy (10)
Frequently Avoids (8–9)	Frequently Avoids (8–9)	Frequently Avoids (8–9)	Frequently Avoids (8–9)	Frequently Avoids (8–9)	Frequently Avoids (8–9)	Frequently Avoids (8–9)	Emotional (8–9)	Always (8–9)	Poor (8–9)
Sometimes Avoids (7–8)	Sometimes Avoids (7–8)	Sometimes Avoids (7–8)	Sometimes Avoids (7–8)	Sometimes Avoids (7–8)	Sometimes Avoids (7–8)	Sometimes Avoids (7–8)	Slow to Warm (7–8)	Occasionally (7–8)	Okay (7–8)
Never Avoids (5–6)	Never Avoids (5–6)	Never Avoids (5–6)	Never Avoids (5–6)	Never Avoids (5–6)	Never Avoids (5–6)	Never Avoids (5–6)	Adaptable (5–6)	Never (5–6)	Proficient (5–6)
Sometimes Seeks (3–4)	Sometimes Seeks (3–4)	Sometimes Seeks (3–4)	Sometimes Seeks (3–4)	Sometimes Seeks (3–4)	Sometimes Seeks (3–4)	Sometimes Seeks (3–4)	Extrovert (3–4)	N/A	Good (3–4)
Always Seeks (1–2)	Always Seeks (1–2)	Always Seeks (1–2)	Always Seeks (1–2)	Always Seeks (1–2)	Always Seeks (1–2)	Always Seeks (1–2)	Difficulty (1–2)	N/A	Superior (1–2)

Figure 3. Thinking tool to judge your family's sensory systems. *Note.* Sensory scores are identified in parentheses.

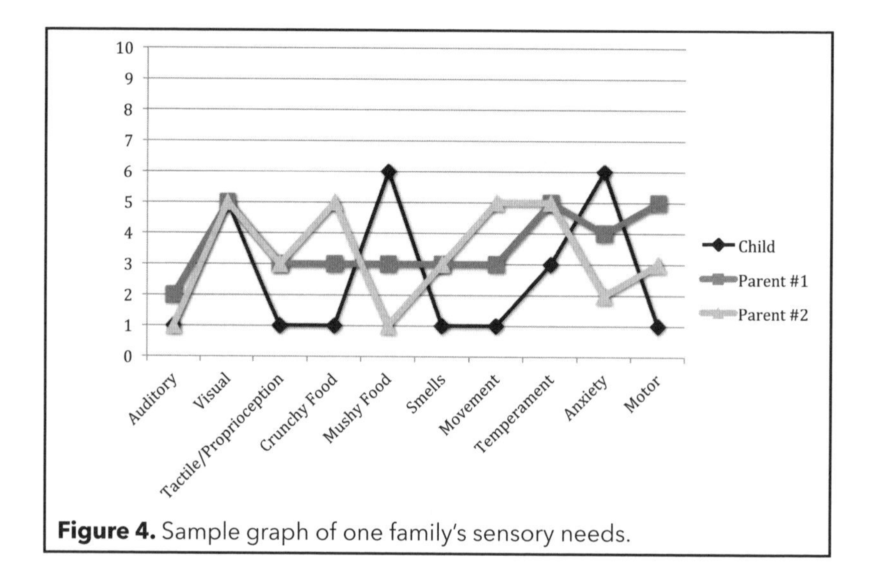

Figure 4. Sample graph of one family's sensory needs.

variety of areas. However, promise arises in the areas of overlap or close correlation (e.g., within the sensory area of auditory).

Now it's time for some self-reflection. Ask yourself these questions:

1. Where are our major differences?
2. Where are our similarities?
3. What am I (and my spouse) willing to change to better fit my child's needs?
4. What is almost impossible to change and requires new habits and routines to meet my child's sensory needs?

SWOT YOUR FAMILY

Another technique we would like you to consider is borrowed from the business world. When assessing an organization, business leaders will often conduct an analysis of the strengths, weaknesses, opportunities, and threats to optimal performance. This is abbreviated as SWOT analysis. As a parent, you are the executive of the family, the conductor of the orchestra, if you will. You raise your baton and conduct the flow of activity. Having data, information about the strengths of the family, where the weaknesses are, what opportunities you have that can help you meet your goals, and a way to anticipate threats (and remove them before they disrupt your life) can be very powerful. Figure 5 provides an example of one family's SWOT analysis. After looking at the example provided, take a few minutes and complete a SWOT analysis for your family in the blank grid provided in Figure 6.

REVIEWING SENSORY ISSUES

To review what we've talked about so far, take another look at the following information:

- Sensory overresponsiveness (SOR) can be a delay or an immaturity in the sensory motor system where a child has behavioral responses to sensory input that are of a greater intensity and for a longer period of time than that of most other children their age.
- Sensory underresponsive (SUR) children often passively respond to the stimuli or disregard the sensory information altogether, therefore seeking a greater amount of sensory input through intensity and duration. This is also known as "poor registration" of sensory stimuli.
- Using problem solving to identify sensory input that can help a child feel "just right" can improve family quality of life (FQoL) and participation in the daily tasks or occupations of your family. Use of the plotting chart and SWOT analysis should be repeated monthly after you've practiced some of the sensory strategies in this book.

Let's take a minute and consider some examples of families who have used some of the activities in this book to improve family quality of life.

CASE STUDY 1: MIXED SENSORY

Ms. Bailey ("Mom") is concerned about her son's poor social skills (i.e., poor sharing, unable to transition from preferred tasks) and sensory issues (i.e., covers ears when around loud sound, touching others incessantly, seeks movement, fearlessness and poor safety awareness), all impacting Chris's occupational roles (i.e., participation on his t-ball team

Strengths Dad is calm. Mom is creative. Uri is a good thinker, likes to solve puzzles.	**Weaknesses** Dad is gone in the mornings and not available to help. Uri wakes up grumpy, refuses to get dressed, says everything is "itchy."
Opportunities: Uri wants to get his green belt in karate, so maybe we can use karate moves to "wake up" our bodies before we have to get dressed? Maybe Uri can help us solve the problem.	**Threats** We seem to always be on a time crunch. Mom's temperament gets overstimulated when Uri screams.

Figure 5. Sample family SWOT analysis.

Strengths	**Weaknesses**
Opportunities:	**Threats**

Figure 6. Blank SWOT grid.

and in the classroom). Mom says she worries when Chris seems unable to stop annoying his brother and friends by "getting in their face," crowding them, and invading their space. Mom refers to Chris as a "sensory kid"; she says he is always distracted, has tantrums, and overreacts all of the time. She has timed his tantrums and even though most people accuse her of exaggeration, she swears Chris can cry and tantrum for 15 minutes at a time if she tries to get him to do something he doesn't want to, like getting dressed in the morning. Chris is clumsy—learning to ride a tricycle took him forever. Chris sat up at a normal age (9–10 months), but he walked a little bit late (18 months). He takes forever to fall asleep at night (sometimes an hour to fall asleep, sometimes he wakes in the night and moves to his parents' bed). This keeps the family awake, meaning they're exhausted in the mornings. Mom says she and Dad are usually on the same page with most parenting decisions, and they are a "team," but they feel overwhelmed by the disruption from Chris's behavioral outbursts and refusal to cooperate with simple routines. Chris does respond to his parents at times and he seems to be motivated to please his Mom and Dad. Mom calls Chris a "drama queen" and says he becomes freaked out all of the time, especially when someone "invades" his personal space, touches him (when he is not forewarned), or if he has to share a toy or something. She finds this particularly confusing because she says Chris is the *king* of space invaders himself! By 4 years old, she feels Chris should be able to hold it together, but he is still acting like a 2-year-old. Mornings are "nightmares" for the family because Chris won't get dressed and she can pretty much count on him to have a tantrum if she tries to hurry him along and out the door for school. The family becomes frustrated and mornings are often full of screaming and emotional outbursts as the parents attempt to discipline Chris—she says she's pulling her hair out and feels really overwhelmed.

In order to help his parents find strategies for Chris, we performed a SWOT analysis for the family (see Figure 7).

Chris has mixed sensory processing. His sensory systems are categorized as SUR and sensation craving (a definite difference from his peers). SUR means that sometimes Chris can have low levels of energy and feel tired and withdrawn. Children with SUR have trouble noticing sensation and often, by the time they do, they can have "too much," indicated as *poor modulation,* such as when Chris throws tantrums over seemingly small things (e.g., the sound of the car radio, clapping). Mom intuitively understands Chris when she reports that Chris's behaviors seem to be "a result of the environment."

Children who fall into the category of sensation craving are active and continuously engaged in their environment; they enjoy and seek sensory input. For example, Chris takes risks with his body without anticipation of the consequences, yet while he enjoys sensation, he cannot modulate it (balance the sensations). Chris exhibits sensory sensitivity

Strengths	**Weaknesses**
Mom and Dad work together. Chris responds well to his parents.	*Sensory Processing* • *auditory processing* (covers ears around noise) • *vestibular processing* (seeks movement to the point of poor safety) • *touch processing* (touches others incessantly) • *modulation of sensory input affecting emotional responses* (prone to tantrums and overreacts a lot) • *proprioceptive processing* (clumsy and learning to ride a tricycle took him forever) *Behavioral and Emotional Responses* • *emotional/social responses* (extremely emotional, especially when someone "invades" his personal space, touches him) • *behavioral outcomes of sensory processing* *Factor* • *sensory seeking* (crowding others and invading their space, unsafe movement, touching others) • *emotionally reactive* (tantrums)
Opportunity Increase sensation to support performance.	**Threats** Chris can be fatigued and refuse strategies if he thinks they will take energy to perform.

Figure 7. SWOT analysis for Chris.

and sensory-avoiding behaviors related to tactile processing, especially in the oral (mouth) area—he overattends and avoids sensation in the oral sensory system. This may contribute, for example, to Chris's rigid behaviors related to the temperature of foods, to avoid mixed textures (such as soup), to refuse to have his face wiped or hair washed, and needing to be forewarned before being touched.

It is not uncommon for children to seek the sensory input they need to regulate or feel "just right" in their bodies, and Chris would benefit from more strategies that will help his system to build tolerance to sensations he perceives to be disturbing.

First, Mom and Dad developed a sensory diet for Chris to support his daily routine at home and at school. They increased opportunities for strong sensory motor activities to help Chris regulate his sensory system and his arousal level. Activities that involve increased proprioceptive input (input to the muscles and tendons surrounding the joints that then help the brain be aware of the position of body parts and how they are moving) such as jumping, pushing, or pulling can increase body awareness, as well help organize the sensory system and contribute to better muscle tone. Activities that involve deep pressure (input received through the tactile system with firm contact to the skin) such as bear hugs, massages, and swimming can be calming and organizing to a sensory system. Here are the activities they began to employ:

- wheelbarrow walks when going to and from the bathroom when brushing teeth;
- jumping from bed to kitchen in the morning;
- carrying heavy objects (e.g., groceries, books) prior to transitions and when shopping with Mom;
- bear walk (on hands and feet, right hand and foot, then left hand and foot) before dinner;
- crab walk (back to floor on hands and feet) after bath; and
- a weekly game night in the evening to foster family fun and turn taking and practice "staying in one's space" during a family friendly, low-risk opportunity.

To increase Chris's performance with dressing, the family has created a routine that includes prepping the body with activities offered to Chris that prepare him for the occupation of dressing. Activities such as "get your shoes and come give Mom a hug" serve as ways to break the task down while providing organizing sensory input to Chris's system; in addition, using "friction treatment" supports Chris as he gets changed from his pajamas (see Activity 2 on p. 48).

CASE STUDY 2: SENSORY UNDERRESPONSIVE ERIN

Erin is a 9-year-old girl who is struggling to get her homework done. Specifically, she avoids spelling and writing and cannot seem to learn her multiplication/math facts. When Mom asks her to sit down and get her homework done, she kicks the chair, puts her head down, chews on her pencil, gets up to get a snack, and eventually cries because, "It's too hard!" Erin is a very capable child and at times, her work is excellent. Mom and Dad are very frustrated and the teacher is concerned as well. Erin has begun to "hate school" and tries to argue that homework is a waste of time, stupid, and child abuse. To support Erin, Mom has a homework area set up and Erin has to sit there until she gets her work done, no matter how long it takes. There are many evenings filled with tears. Mom is even concerned that sometimes her daughter seems almost depressed—lethargic, uninterested, and underexcited by the activites that most kids would find fun and pleasurable.

After consultation with an occupational therapist, Erin's Mom and Dad realized they could think differently about what was going on. This realization gave them new "lenses" through which to view Erin's behavior and made them excited to try a new approach. Here's what the OT explained to Erin's Mom and Dad:

> From a sensory integrative perspective, learning occurs when a person receives accurate sensory information, processes it, and uses it to organize behaviors. When an individual receives inaccurate or unreliable sensory input, then her ability to process the information and create responses is disrupted. Poor sensory processing can take the form of overresponsivity, such as becoming agitated when someone brushes against you, or underresponsivity, such as needing to be tapped on the shoulder several times to gain attention. Proprioceptive input refers to information from our muscles and joints and provides feedback to allow us to know where our body is, where it is moving, and how much force is being used. Inefficiencies in processing, modulating,

> and integrating sensory input and neurodevelopmental maturation can require us to expend greater effort in completing motor tasks, may contribute to frustration, can contribute to poor behavioral responses, and may result in difficulty with more complex and novel tasks. Because we create sensations for ourselves, behavior guides what sensory input we need.
>
> Erin needs more sensory input to feel "alert," so we're going to increase the sensation for her throughout the day. Individuals who have SUR tend to appear uninterested and can have flat or dull affect (facial expression and emotional reaction). Individuals with poor registration have low energy levels and can act as if they are overly tired and can be prone to depression. The rationale for this, using the sensory processing model, is that the brain is not getting what it needs to generate responses, and the child's tendency to respond in accordance with high thresholds leads to an apathetic, self-absorbed appearance. It is hypothesized that children with poor registration have inadequate neural activation to support sustained performance and therefore may miss salient cues in the context to support ongoing responsivity.

Mom and Dad began to see the OT might be right—once they considered that Erin's behaviors might be due to poor attention, poor arousal during school tasks, and poor ability to organize and complete assignments because her nervous system just wasn't receiving enough input to maintain functional levels of alertness, they intuitively were able to use different strategies to help Erin. They were especially concerned about the link between depression and SUR.

As the OT explained to them, individuals who have poor registration tend to appear uninterested and can have flat or dull affect (facial expression and emotional reaction). This appears to be the primary presenting problem for Erin. Individuals with poor registration have low energy levels and can act as if they are overly tired, especially when not sufficiently stimulated by their environment. She explained that if we look at Erin wearing sensory processing lenses, then we can imagine her brain is not getting what it needs to create a response, so when she needs a lot of information/input before her brain pays attention (i.e., to respond in accordance with high thresholds), she can look apathetic or self-absorbed, but really, the input hasn't gotten the brain's attention yet. It is hypothesized that children with poor registration have inadequate neural activation to support sustained performance and therefore may miss salient cues in the context to support ongoing responsivity. A child with poor registration, as is seen in Erin's case, must have sufficient sensorimotor input to result in alert states for learning to occur. She may then be motivated to participate in learning opportunities, develop increased social skills with increased social interactions, and develop a bigger repertoire of skills because she is engaged in more occasions for learning to take place. She needs more input than others in order for her system to realize or register the input. Therefore, movement, deep pressure, and frequent change in the direction of Erin's body in space will be helpful for her to reach and maintain a level of alertness sufficient for learning and engagement to occur.

Erin's parents used the WISE strategy to help determine Erin's sensory needs:

- **W: What is the problem?** Erin has difficulty maintaining sufficient levels of alertness to get her homework done.
- **I: Isolate what you know and what you need to know.** Mom knows Erin likes cold foods, sour tastes, and music. She doesn't know what movement activities might be helpful.
- **S: Strategize.** Mom and Dad consulted with each other and decided that a sensory diet would be a place to start. They also concentrated on using activities from the school chapter (see Chapter 6) in this book and found several they could easily try.
- **E: Evaluate your plan.** The family identified learning math facts and getting homework done in a timely manner as the "solution" they would measure. Because Erin can now get her work done and there is laughing instead of tears, they've evaluated the plan to be successful. Now they're ready to try some activities to help with bedtime!

Some of the strategies Erin's parents tried included:

- Mom and Erin worked together to develop a sensory diet. Each day, Erin gets a bottle of cold water (in a sports water bottle) with lemon. She also has pretzels or another very crunchy snack—one of her favorites is a very cold apple cut up in chunks. Mom prepares these for Erin, and she can help herself.
- Learning math facts while performing jumping jacks has been fun and has helped Erin to maintain her alert state so she could focus and learn. Erin invented her own "Power Up!" to this strategy—she likes to do her jumping jacks while bouncing on a mini-trampoline. Mom joins in and gets a bit of exercise too, which has reduced her stress. There is a lot of laughing during homework time now.
- Erin likes to have music on when she does homework. Before, Mom and Dad reduced all distractions, but now they realize Erin needs sensation to attend. Her iPod playlist for homework time includes the soundtrack from *Mortal Kombat* and the song *Party in the USA*.

> We are going to provide Power Ups! in the book, ways to take one activity and up the challenge by making it super-potent! You will see that a Power Up! is provided for every activity and, if you're lucky to have a kid like Erin, he or she will help you think of more Power Ups! than even *we* could imagine!
>
> You can use the Morning and Evening Routine samples and blank charts in Appendix A, pages 145–148, to help your child create a strategy to try that will work for the whole family.

CASE STUDY 3: OVERRESPONSIVE PAUL

Paul avoids playing with the other children on the playground, stating, "They are too noisy and I'm afraid of them, they might bump me." Paul appears to be sensitive to sensation. He is "overly sensitive" at times to the point of being afraid of sensation. Sometimes Paul "tunes out" during activities. He recently ran away from school after a fire drill, got stuck in a hole, and refused to come out. His one friend, Robin, was able to convince Paul to return to the classroom but Paul continues to be afraid that the bells might ring again. Paul is trying to keep sensory events at bay that he finds to be overwhelming, but his strategy is to withdraw or run away, taking him away from social opportunities and play experiences.

Paul attempts to protect himself from stimuli that he finds "overwhelming" or otherwise "frightening" by either withdrawing or engaging in an emotional outburst that enables him to get out of the threatening situation. Individuals who are avoiding sensation also might create rituals for their daily lives, and by their behavior, entice others to support these rituals. For example, Paul frequently has a good morning getting ready for school if he awakens in a certain way, eats a certain breakfast food (honey and peanut butter), and if his mom allows him to wear certain clothing items (a well-worn, tight cotton shirt). Paul has a bad day if that ritual is altered. His parents have learned what constitutes a good day and attempt to recreate it each day to facilitate getting Paul ready for school. This ritual may include engaging in intense interests such as playing with kites or insisting on singing a favorite song. From a behavioral perspective, Paul seems stubborn or controlling. However, from a sensory processing perspective, he is trying his best to limit his sensory inputs to those that are familiar and therefore easy for his nervous system to interpret. Individuals who avoid sensation are resistant to changes because change represents an opportunity to be bombarded with unfamiliar (and potentially harmful or painful) stimuli. Withdrawal or tuning out is often used as a coping behavior when an individual feels overwhelmed by or does not understand the demands being placed upon him. Individuals who have SOR (see next case study) tend to be distractible in the areas of sensitivity. They might be overly cautious about proceeding in some situations because they missed something (while being distracted), or might become upset either by their own difficulties with tracking tasks or with others who are interrupting them, or might be aware of every stimulus that becomes available without the commensurate abilities to habituate to these stimuli or filter out extraneous stimuli. These areas of sensitivity may be overwhelming to the system at times and create a need for an individual to withdraw as a way of modulating the sensory input.

Taking a WISE approach, Paul's parents have identified the following concerns:

- **W: What is the problem?** The parents will ask, "What seems to be getting in the way of Paul's ability to participate?" For example, they might say, "Paul seems overwhelmed by sensory input."

- **I: Isolate what you know and what you need to know.** What seems to work? That's a clue that will help the parents come up with a potential solution. For example, Mom and Dad know Paul has a good morning getting ready for school if they stick to a rigid ritual and in contrast, Paul has a bad day if that ritual is altered. That gives them some good information and ideas for a strategy.
- **S: Strategize.** What can Mom and Dad try? We might imagine Mom and Dad begin to identify ways to have a schedule but also to provide Paul with socially appropriate ways to limit sensory input while exploring new sensations in a slow, deliberate way. For example, could they post a schedule that Paul helps them create? And then plan, in advance, one new thing to try, adding it to the schedule? Maybe adding music to the morning routine (something Paul likes) would work—it would be a new sensation, one that Paul finds pleasurable, and little by little he will learn that new isn't always bad.
- **E: Evaluate your plan.** If Paul's parents created a chart to track the changes they hope to see—fewer meltdowns in the morning routine and more willingness to play with friends at recess—they can evaluate the effectiveness of their WISE approach.

CASE STUDY 4: SENSATION CRAVING TINA

Tina likes bouncing in the classroom, making nonproductive comments (a favorite is "oo-hoo-hoo-hoo"!), frequently touching other children, and repeatedly shouting, "I'm the only one like me!" Tina craves sensory input. She frequently needs to be asked to come down from the top of the climbing structures on the playground, remove her hands/arms from peers whom she squeezes too hard, and has been in the office five times in the last 2 weeks for bounding toward a friend and, consequently, knocking her to the ground. Her teacher says, "Kids like Tina, but I'm worried—her way of expressing friendship is frequently misunderstood and kids are afraid she will hurt them again." Children with sensory seeking patterns may appear hyperactive, unaware of touch or pain, touch others too often, engage in unsafe behaviors (such as climbing too high), or enjoy sounds that are too loud. Individuals who have a sensation seeking style of processing information are active and continuously engaged in their environments. These individuals add sensory input to every experience in daily life. They make noises while working, fidget, rub, or explore objects with their skin, chew on things, and wrap body parts around furniture or people as a way to increase input during tasks. They may appear excitable or seem to lack consideration for safety while playing. Performance problems are related to the interference of their seeking behaviors to ongoing performance and they need to have sensory input incorporated into their daily routines so they don't have to stop what they're doing to stay alert. Tina's mom and dad have been using sensory activities that she likes (e.g., jumping on the trampoline, playing on the swing, dancing and singing when doing homework) as rewards, encouraging her to calm down and "earn" a turn do to something she enjoys.

What is the problem? Tina craves sensory input to feel "just right" but doesn't seem able to match her need for sensation to the environment. Her mom and dad have been withholding sensation, which sets up a problem for Tina—they know they need to help her get more organized. After working with an occupational therapist, they now understand that it is important instead to use sensory strategies that are helpful to support Tina in getting the input *first* and enabling her better performance.

What do you think they can do?

W____

____

I____

____

S____

____

E _______________________________________

____

Your turn: Write your own case and apply the WISE approach to problem solve for your child.

What are the problems you are experiencing with your child?

___

___

What time of day are the challenges more disruptive?

___

___

What activities seem to make things worse? Can you see a pattern?

___

___

What activities seem to help? Can you see a pattern?

___

___

What activity would you like to try? How will you know if it has helped your family?

___

___

Make a plan—write the activity, the page number, and your timeline below.

___

___

CASE STUDY 5: USING AN ACTIVITY DIARY WITH JUSTIN

Justin is a 7-year-old boy. He presents with sensory overresponsivity. This is particularly seen in tactile input. Due to his reactions to sensory input, he often appears overaroused. Justin's mother has difficulty getting him to eat a variety of food. He loves pizza and French fries, but not much of anything else. Justin has trouble getting to sleep at night and will sometimes only get a few hours of rest. This makes him irritable, posing a huge challenge during the morning routine.

Other challenging routines are homework time and social interaction. Justin takes a long time getting to his homework and completing it. His mother has tried a reward system that does not appear to work. During play dates, Justin does not interact with the other children without a lot of prompting. He has expressed anxiety over the unpredictable behavior of other children. In addition, the other boys love messy play, something Justin avoids. In response, Justin's mother has incorporated some of the sensory activities in this book into their routine. She used a diary to track his progress and reaction to the stimuli. Figure 8 shares Justin's activity diary. After reading it over, think about your own child and the activities that might help him or her. Consider each of the senses: olfactory, vestibular, proprioception, tactile, auditory, visual, and gustatory. Also, think about the sensory motor system and how praxis can be incorporated into daily routines to promote greater function and ease of movement during activities.

Child: Justin **Date:** Monday, October 7, 2013

Activity	**Time** *(When Was the Activity Performed)?*	**Duration** *(For How Long Was It Performed?)*	**Arousal Level Prior to Input** *(High, Low, Calm, Alert)*	**Change in Reaction?** *(Yes or No)*
Vestibular				
Sushi Roll (see p. 163)	Before school and before homework	5 minutes each	High	Yes; after sushi roll, finished homework in one hour.
Proprioception/Oral Motor				
1. Post Office (see p. 157)	Before dinner	About 3 minutes	High	Ate two spoonfuls of mashed potatoes! That's a first!
2. Hills and Valleys (see p. 164)	Before bedtime	5 minutes	Calm	Not at first but fell asleep one hour sooner than yesterday.
Tactile				
Go Fishing (see p. 73)	Before play date	About 10 minutes	Alert	He was very cautious at first, then excited when he found the fish! We did another round with his friend.

Figure 8. Justin's activity diary.

Part II

52 Week-by-Week Activities to Restore Sanity to Your Family Life

Chapter 4
Morning Routines

Mornings are hectic for families. Children need to get up, get dressed, have breakfast, and organize their school supplies. Developing habits and routines that allow for smooth orchestration of these activities is the key to a low-stress, smooth start of a day. The short time frame for many morning routines can exacerbate family stress. But when a child has difficulty making a plan, moving his body in a coordinated fashion, or tolerating changes in sensation, his behavior can disrupt the whole family and send them all into a day kicked off with stress and chaos. Establishing routines, providing sensations that help organize the child's (and parents') nervous system, and helping parents build a toolkit of strategies all dampen down chaos and improve participation in life, an essential foundation to QoL in the mornings. Just like the nervous system plays a role in our behavior, what we do with our bodies can have a direct influence on what goes in our nervous system. What normally poses a challenge for us can actually be a tool for our success! Sensory behavior plays a large role in limiting family participation. In order to be successful, families can use strategies throughout the day that help them manage the child's and family's routines (Schaff et al., 2011).

Take just one morning task, brushing your teeth. Brushing your teeth seems like a simple task, but the feel of the brush, the taste of the toothpaste, and the invasion of sensation to the mouth can be extremely overwhelming for some children. The National Museum of Dentistry has developed a guide that provides both sensory- and behavior-based strategies for parents to use that will help them effectively teach lifelong oral health routines (this guide can be found at http://www.amchp.org/programsandtopics/CYSHCN/projects/spharc/Documents/autism_dental_from_national_museum_of_dentistry1.pdf).

Mealtime is another area that can be a challenging time for children with delays in development. There are many different types of food that a child may find unpleasant due to the sensory characteristics of taste, smell, or texture. In addition to morning meals, parents often report that asking their child to get dressed in the morning is a real struggle. Some children are very sensitive to certain fabrics, while other children's nervous systems are underaroused in the morning and they can't seem to generate enough energy to attend to and follow through on the multi-stepped task of getting underwear, shirt, shoes, and pants or skirts on in a timely manner. The strategies presented on pages 47–60 are aimed at this time of day, the morning routine.

ACTIVITY 1

RED LIGHT! GREEN LIGHT!

This activity can help to wake up the nervous system and get us ready for the day. Learning to attend to a cue in the environment (e.g., listen, look, smell, etc.) and respond with the body in a timely manner is a critical skill. Incorporating this activity into morning routines can prove to be a very helpful strategy.

DIRECTIONS

Tell your child, "When I say 'green light,' you run over to the dresser and get out your socks, shirt, and pants. If I say 'red light,' then you have to freeze. Ready?"

Randomly stop and start the child as he or she sequences the tasks of getting dressed.

POWER UP!

"Mother, May I?" is a similar game that will make a child listen and attend to the speaker. It also helps make listening and following directions a fun game. To start the game, the child makes a request of the parent: "Mother, may I take 20 bites of this banana?" The parent can reply "Yes, you may," or "No, you may not." If the answer is no, then the caregiver can modify the number of times the child can do the desired task.

In addition to "Mother, May I?," Freeze Dance is a game that challenges your child's ability to initiate and terminate movements on cue. You play a song and while the music plays, you all wave your arms and wiggle—or, if you like, everyone cleans up the dishes or the floor—and when the music stops, everyone has to freeze. In this moment, you can give an instruction: "Freeze! Are you frozen? When you unfreeze, it's time to get your shoes on," or whatever the next thing is on the family's agenda.

ACTIVITY 2

FRICTION TREATMENT

Changing temperature is alerting to the nervous system. Think of yourself walking outside on a brisk morning—brrr, you are stimulated to wake up! For an immature nervous system, changing temperature by taking off a child's pajamas can be as alerting as stepping outside on a bitter cold day. To dampen this sensation and make changing clothes easier, offer deep pressure to the skin, rubbing off the light touch/temperature change.

DIRECTIONS

Tell your child: "It's time to take off those pajamas and get your shirt on—I'm ready with your friction treatment. Ready, set, go!"

Once the new shirt is on, rub the child's back, arms, and tummy vigorously, applying friction to the skin. Think about adding a silly song ("I'm gonna rub, rub, rub, rub, rub that tickle away, oh yeah!") or say in a loudish voice, "FRICTION TREATMENT! 10, 9, 8, 7, 6, 5, 4, 3, 2, 1, now pants!"

Deep pressure is very helpful to rub out the tickly touch sensations, itching, and discomfort from a change in temperature. Think about what you do when you go outside—if it's cold, you instinctively rub briskly on your arm/skin. The friction treatment technique uses the same principle to help children adjust.

One great thing about kids is that they care more about you being playful than whether or not you are singing on key or creating impressive lyrics. Be as silly as you can and remember, friction is a force of Mother Nature!

ACTIVITY 3

COCOON AND BUTTERFLY

Providing deep pressure (tactile input) and proprioception (input to the joints and muscles) can help children feel more centered or organized in their bodies.

DIRECTIONS

When it's time to get out of bed, wrap your child tight in her blanket, like a cocoon. Twist a hand hold in the blanket and hang on tight. Imagine that your hand is a giant binder clip—you are keeping the blanket on and holding the child steady as she walks through the house. When you reach your destination, have your child "emerge" by pushing and pulling herself free of the blanket and floating to the kitchen table for her breakfast.

POWER UP!

Let two children snuggle up together!

ACTIVITY 4

BREAKFAST FOODS

Most of us think of food at breakfast in terms of the nutritional content, but our bodies also need sensory nutrition in the morning. Some foods help us feel calm, others can help us wake up and provide rich sensory motor experiences to the mouth. Think about the texture, temperature, and consistency of food and plan breakfasts that support your child's sensory patterns. Engage your child in planning the meals. If food is an area of extreme rigidity, add other sensory experiences to support successful participation. The child can pick out what he or she wants to eat for breakfast the evening before so that the morning routine will have a greater chance of running smoothly.

Don't forget about temperature! Breakfast ice cream? Frozen fruit smoothies? Have the child help the night before with adding fruit to yogurt, then freezing to assist with true sensory seekers. Children who do not appear to feel pain may need an intense meal to start their day. Also, consider using spicy foods such as spicy green eggs and ham. Or have your child clean out the bottom of his cereal bowl using a straw to suck it dry.

Here are some sensational breakfast ideas:

- **Visual/Gustatory.** Eat a rainbow—select one food for each color in the rainbow (e.g., a fruit cup with banana, blueberries, strawberries, mandarin oranges, and green grapes).
- **Proprioception/Tactile.** Try adding extra crunch to the meal—add nuts to cereal, select cereals that are highly crunchy, or add chopped apples to cereal or serve them on the side with yogurt dip. Sucking sensations also help with this area; provide a straw for milk or even yogurt!
- **Olfactory.** Have a favorite smell at the breakfast table—think about roses on the table, vanilla or peppermint oil on a cotton ball to sniff between bites, or lemon slices to scent the room. Your child could also hold a scented stuffed animal on his lap as he eats.
- **Auditory.** Add music to breakfast time by playing something to wake up the system. Music with string instruments can be very alerting, while music with heavy bass tones is

ACTIVITY 4, *CONTINUED*

grounding. Think about the soundtrack from *Star Wars* or *Tarzan* to get the body awake!

- **Vestibular.** Dance with your child in the morning or take a walk. Consider wearing a carpenter's belt (one with pockets). You can pack a granola bar and a yogurt/fruit smoothie and snack for your child to enjoy while you take a quick walk around the neighborhood or march through your house. To increase vestibular input, play 20 questions—when your child shakes her head yes or no, she is stimulating her vestibular system!

You can plan a sensational eating experience for your child. Think about packing your child's lunch box with a sensory frame of mind. Include a straw for him to use to eat when he eats his applesauce or yogurt. Provide chewy foods like dried blueberries, beef jerky, or bagels. Toss in a good dose of crunchy foods like carrots, apple chips, or dried strawberries. Yummy!

ACTIVITY 5

PACK A POWERFUL LUNCH

Chores give a child the opportunity to learn good habits, to practice frustration tolerance, and to help the family. One chore children with sensory issues can take on is helping with meal preparation. Even very young children can pack their own lunches with a bit of help from a parent. Being organized is the key.

DIRECTIONS

When you come home from the store, have your child open packages of cookies, beef jerky, or other lunch items and create individual portions by filling multiple snack-sized plastic bags. Organize these by sensation—a section for crunchy foods, salty foods, juicy foods, chewy foods, juice boxes with straws, foods to eat with a straw (like applesauce), and so on. In the morning, your child can pack her lunch

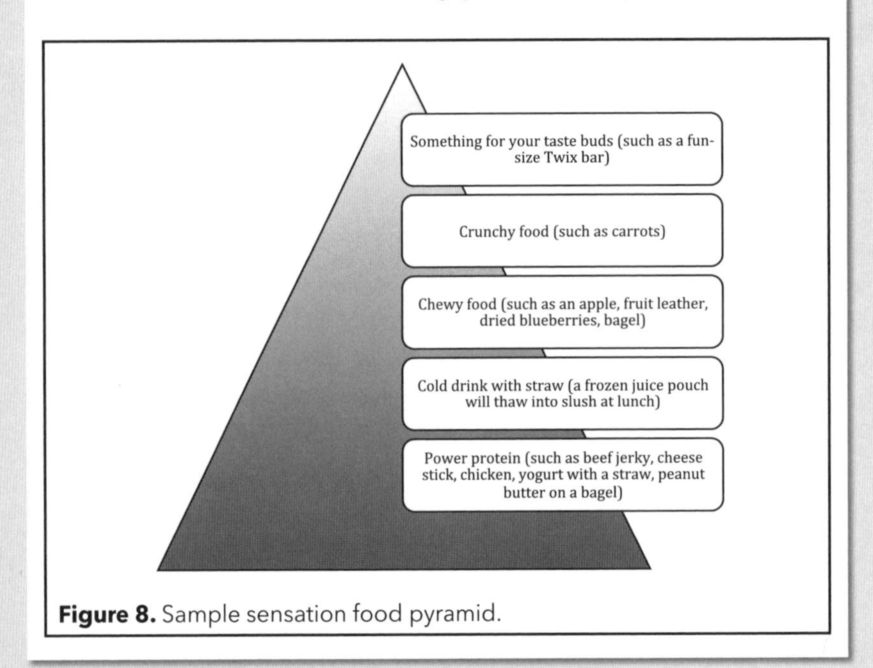

Figure 8. Sample sensation food pyramid.

ACTIVITY 5, *CONTINUED*

by selecting one of each item. Post a sensation food pyramid like the one in Figure 8 for her to use as a guide. (See Appendix A, p. 139 for a blank pyramid for you and your family to complete and post.)

You can make a list of foods that match the nutritional pyramid and the sensory pyramid with your child and post it on the pantry door. Some items meet multiple categories. We like to play a game called "Bang for the Buck" and see how many foods we can pack that meet two or more criteria!

ACTIVITY 6

TEETH TIME

We know our children should brush and floss their teeth at least twice a day—along with having regular dental visits—if they are to have a healthy mouth. We know good oral health is important for our child's overall health. But when a simple action like brushing teeth devolves into a daily tantrum, families choose their battles. Your child may have a mouth sensitivity that makes brushing and flossing especially challenging for him. Motor delays can make it difficult for a child to move the brush around in his mouth without hitting and injuring those sensitive tissues. What to do?

Put on a "power suit" before brushing. When it's time to brush, wrap your child in a blanket or put on a heavy cape (see Appendix B, p. 151, for instructions on making one of these). Deep pressure is helpful to the nervous system and can help us tolerate sensation that is otherwise overwhelming.

If your child's mouth is undersensitive, you can try waking up the mouth first. Consider mouthwash that you keep in the fridge—remember that cold input is alerting! You can have your child try a swish-swish with the mouthwash to wake up the mouth, then have him brush and spit, and you're on your way! Electric toothbrushes provide vibration to the gums, which is a form of proprioception; some families find this helpful. You will want to slowly build up to this by first using a vibrating infant teether, a regular toothbrush, a battery-operated toothbrush, and then the most stimulating electric toothbrush. You can find more strategies in the Healthy Smiles

ACTIVITY 6, *CONTINUED*

for Autism brochure found at http://www.amchp.org/programsandtopics/CYSHCN/projects/spharc/Documents/autism_dental_from_national_museum_of_dentistry1.pdf.

Sometimes the oddest things make a difference. For Rondalyn's older son, who was very sensitive to taste and touch in the mouth, brushing his teeth was a very difficult activity and a potential battle each morning. Finally, she asked him, "Zac, what do you think I could do that would help you brush your teeth each morning?" He said, "Mom, if I had a timer that looked like a hamburger, and some toothpaste that isn't mint, I think I could do it." Well, she found a timer that looked like a hamburger at a cooking store, and she discovered toothpastes that were fennel and strawberry flavored (both made by Tom's of Maine). For years, Rondalyn's family set that timer and never had a problem again. Zac used Tom's all through middle school, and sometime in high school he transitioned to Arm and Hammer toothpaste. You just have to go with whatever works, so take a minute and problem solve with your child!

ACTIVITY 7

SUPER GROVER

(Note: This is an advanced game, be ready for a workout!)

You've probably played the helicopter game with your small child. You lie on your back, extend your legs and arms, hold the child's hands, and place your feet on her tummy. You lift her into the air, resting your child on your huge feet, still holding onto her hands. This is a great vestibular and proprioceptive activity. But, we can increase the input by transforming the game a bit.

DIRECTIONS

For this activity, the parent lies on the bed (you need some padding). Place 2–4 pillows on *your* tummy. Following the rules for helicopter, hold your child's hands and with your feet, lift her into the air. But then, just like Super Grover falls and crashes out of the sky, let go and let your child fall straight down, landing on the pile of pillows protecting your body (watch for your stomach, chin, and maybe your face!). Repeat until one or both of you have had enough of the input! Add counting down loudly (10, 9, 8 . . .) and release your child on a predictable number if she is overly sensitive. Count and release her on an unpredictable number if she is the kind of kid who needs *lots* of sensory input. Get all of those sillies out during this activity and then, it's time for serious business (like breakfast).

POWER UP!

You can set up a crash pit in the house. Pile up lots of pillows and make sure there are no corners to hit and no way to miss the pillow pit. Your child can run and crash into the pillows over and over. Consider adding this to your morning or bedtime routines. Add a cape and a story about Superman or Super Grover and you will have a routine that is a hit (in more ways than one).

ACTIVITY 8

TWISTY DANCE AND CLUTTER BUSTING

The Twist will *never* go out of style as long as there are kids in the world. Dance with your children in the morning to help them shake out their arms and legs and wake up their bodies. You can do the Twist as directed below or try out our "clutter busting" style of dancing.

DIRECTIONS

To help kids learn to do the Twist, give them this scenario:

> Imagine you are stepping on and trying to put out a small fire under each foot or trying to grind a nut into the ground for a squirrel to find later. Keep the ball of your foot on the ground but lift your heels slightly so you can twist on the balls of your feet. Let your bottom twist in the opposite direction from your knees as you twist from side to side, keeping your feet parallel!

Add on any hand movements or craziness. Have your child hold onto a towel and rub his back with it while he's moving his feet. Put on some great music, such as the original song (here's

ACTIVITY 8, *CONTINUED*

the YouTube link for Chubby Checker and the Twist: http://www.youtube.com/watch?v=xbK0C9AYMd8).

Want to update your moves? Once your kids get down the Twist, have them try new dance styles instead. One is the popular Gangnam Style (you can see a video here: http://www.youtube.com/watch?v=9bZkp7q19f0).

How can dancing get your clutter busted? While you're twisting around the room, stoop and pick up all of the clothes on the floor and toss them into the laundry hamper. Or have your child dance through the house picking up all of the books for the library, wiping down the counters, squirting the cabinets with a spray bottle with cleaner (check the scent first!). We like to assign different tasks to each family member.

Children enjoy making games out of ordinary things. Whenever someone spills something liquid, grab a towel, toss it on the spill, step on it, and do the Twist!

ACTIVITY 9

MAGIC CARPET RIDES

Lethargy in the morning—we can all relate. Wouldn't it be great if someone scooped you up and carried you to work? Morning routines are the work of childhood, as children are learning to organize and get all of their tasks accomplished on someone else's schedule. A magic carpet can come to the rescue. You can also create a Caterpillar Tunnel to use for this activity (directions for creating a Caterpillar Tunnel can be found in Appendix B, p. 154).

DIRECTIONS

Pick a nice cozy blanket and spread it out on the floor by your child's bed. Invite your child to crawl on—be fun in your mood as you climb on board too; remember, you're his best role model. Once on, give the child a few wrap ups (tightly roll him in the blanket and squeeze), making the noise of a motor starting.

Ready for takeoff? Ask the child to hold on (squeeze the blanket with his hands) and off you pull. You can go as fast or slow as your child's sensory system prefers. If you have a pillow pit in the kitchen, consider a crash landing when you arrive. Be ready, though, sometimes one ride isn't enough! If you get too tired, siblings can pull each other. Only children can pull their stuffed animals or other heavy toys.

POWER UP!

Stories are important for children. Consider the storyline that the carpet will only fly for kids in clothes. Hand your child his clothes for the day while he's still in bed. If he gets dressed and climbs on before the carpet flies away, he can have a ride to the kitchen!

ACTIVITY 10

ONE-MINUTE SENSATIONAL CHORES

Consider a 27 fling boogie (adapted from Fly Lady, see http://www.flylady.com) to help your household chores get accomplished.

DIRECTIONS

Turn on some music (high energy music works best). Give each member of your family a trash bag and send him or her through the house to collect 27 items of trash. Once each person is done, he or she tosses the bag in the trash can and is free to move on to his next choice of activity. This works well for other chores also. For example, you can substitute a laundry bag for a trash bag and get dirty clothes collected or take the activity outside and pick up yard debris.

POWER UP!

Make a chores chart of all of the tasks a family member can do in 1-2 minutes. Assign one each day to each family member. Your goal is family well-being and quality of life. If the family achieves 90% of the Power Up!, then everyone gets a family reward like dessert first or extra free time. Consider setting up a Chore Wars account (a free online positive game for community well-being as related to the accomplishment of chores; check it out at http://www.chorewars.com).

Chapter 5

Mealtime Routines

Food has centralized importance in our lives and sharing time together often includes routines associated with food. We care for others with food, making sandwiches in the shape of small triangles, heating up soup when loved ones are sick, serving cookies at the end of a fantastic family barbeque, or sharing seasonal foods that are rich with tradition. Problem behaviors during mealtimes can be a source of stress for families and a barrier to quality in the relationships as well as impaired family enjoyment. Food rituals, including taboo foods, serve as a unifier for families and create cohesion. Food can be considered a marker of social boundaries as well—perhaps your family always eats at the table together or you always say a prayer before eating or share one thing you are grateful for. Perhaps your family would never eat certain foods for religious, health, or moral reasons. One family may have the established routine that the children cannot have sweets; another family may be indulgent, with sweets offered liberally. Habits and routines promote acceptance and avoidance of many foods.

Food is a sensory experience—tastes, smells, textures, sound. This can also be a source of pleasure. Some foods are only served on special occasions, prepared by one person or associated with holidays, seasons, certain family members or friends: Grandma Maggie makes Monkey

Bread and hot rolls, Grandma Hilda bakes molasses cookies, Dad grills in the summer, Uncle Stefan makes the Thanksgiving turkey. Food is linked to festivities and can mark special occasions. Intentionally eating together creates time and space to engage on spiritual and intellectual levels unique to human beings, cultivates community, and perpetuates relationships.

Mealtimes help us establish family traditions and develop a sense of order. We use mealtimes to reinforce family values and traditions: Share, say please, clean your plate, say excuse me, take turns talking, being grateful. The relationship between family rituals, family routines, and health has been shown to be a protective factor for families and correlates with FQoL, improving a sense of belonging and place, creating family identity, improving family communication, and providing an opportunity for incidental learning. However, sensory motor difficulties can become barriers to participation in mealtime routines. Sometimes, a child's avoidance behaviors can grow quite extreme and need specialized treatment. Many occupational therapists or speech therapists have specialized training to help a child with extremely dysfunctional eating behaviors, and although that level of impairment is beyond the scope of this book, treatment for food selectivity may be more effective if consideration/treatment of sensory overresponsivity or underresponsivity is included in the protocol (Suarez, Nelson, & Curtis, 2012).

Eating meals together as a family is a protective factor, setting up a cascade of positive outcomes for the child. Families who have frequent meals together see benefits such as enhanced vocabulary in children, greater academic success, healthier food selectivity, and even avoidance of high-risk behaviors (e.g., substance abuse, sexual activity, depression/suicide, violence, school problems, binge eating/purging; Crespo, Kielpikowski, Pryor, & Jose, 2011; Dengel, n.d.).

Barriers to positive experiences around mealtimes include overly busy schedules, disabilities, and poor fit between a child's internal eating schedule and the family's. Being flexible about when, where, and what you serve your family, making meals fun, involving everyone in food preparation, and encouraging conversation are known supports for better family meals. The activities on the pages that follow will help you make mealtime a success.

ACTIVITY 11

SLUG NIGHT

A slug is a creature without bones that slithers and slides across floors and leaves a trail of ooze. Imagine if you were a family of slugs! You would be draped across the couch with the absolute worst posture and have little energy to get much done. You can issue "Slug Night Coupons," allowing each family member to call for a "Slug Night" every now and then.

Foods served during slug night are no-prep foods and might include cold leftovers, pizza delivered to your door, or other take-out food–the key is that no one does much work. Your family gets to eat in front of a TV show, while playing a game, or nestled inside a blanket or a sleeping bag while you each lie around on the floor–something "sluggy" or slothlike.

Slug night promotes an atmosphere of ease around food and can break up a routine that is associated with battling the child. Children benefit from the fun and relaxation and family cohesion will almost always be a notable outcome! Slug night also can provide a change in routine that is pleasant and therefore promotes flexibility and openness to new routines.

Camping can be relaxing, and many kids enjoy eating and sleeping outdoors in a tent under the stars. But *getting* to the campsite (i.e., packing, lugging what you need, hiking) can be a chore. Why not have a sluggish indoor camping trip? Pitch a tent or create a tent with blankets and chairs right in your living room. Open up a picnic basket with cold chicken, crawl in your sleeping bags, turn out the lights, flick on those flashlights, and enjoy being a camp sloth right in your own home. You could hide puzzle pieces under couch cushions or in pillows and then have the family assemble the puzzle in the tent. You might also consider hiding dinner! What if you had to search to find the bag of chips (hidden behind a chair maybe?) and a jar of salsa (tucked under the couch pillow) or fixings for s'mores hidden about, and so on? You can have so much fun with an indoor picnic or camping trip and, if you like, it can be practice for the real event in the future.

ACTIVITY 12

THERABAND CHAIRS

Chairs are an opportunity for sensory support. Kids figure this out and lean back, sit sideways, and scoot the chair back and forth. We can observe this behavior and understand that they are attempting to achieve better attention or sensory arousal by seeking sensation that we know the nervous system uses to help us feel alert and attentive. Fortunately, as adults, we can help a child select more adaptive strategies than the ones in their limited repertoire.

Therabands or exercise bands are available in the exercise section of large box stores such as Target or Walmart. Imagine a large rubber band, about 4 feet long. You can use this for exercise, but we like to use it for support on chairs too.

DIRECTIONS

Wrap the theraband around the legs of your child's chair. Tie it tightly. When she sits at the dinner table, she can rest her feet on the band or wrap her legs into the band and pull or push quietly. Remember, pulling or pushing on joints and muscles helps to organize or calm the sensory system, especially when the system is challenged (like when having to smell cauliflower or other strong mealtime smells).

POWER UP!

Make sure your child's feet touch the floor or a stable surface. Having our feet dangle can be uncomfortable. When a child has a sensory motor delay, she often has less ability to maintain her seated posture. Consider making a "table box." Find a box that is the right size to push up under the child's chair so that her feet can rest on the top. You can decorate the box and consider tucking busy box items inside–crayons, a coloring book, puzzles, scented or weighted animals, stress balls, or small toys that would be appropriate to have at the table during dinner.

ACTIVITY 13

LAP DOG

Heavy weight on our skin helps us feel calm. Before coming to the table, let your child choose a weighted friend to help feel calm and ready for participating with your family. Any stuffed animal will do for this activity, but a floppy fellow will be best of all.

After a short outpatient surgical procedure (see Appendix B, p. 153 for full directions) your child's new buddy will have gained a little weight (about 5–10 pounds, to be precise). Filled with fish gravel, this new pet can lie quietly on your child's lap or around her shoulders to help everyone feel a bit more peaceful at mealtime.

POWER UP!

Temperature is a sensation transmitted through the same pathway as tactile information. You can use this to promote greater resilience in the tactile system when a child is overly sensitive or underregistering to textures. Start meals with something cold and provide a straw for added proprioceptive input. Instead of a weighted animal, think about a rice buddy that you warm up and allow your child to hold in his lap during dinner. Or get out the heavy power cape to help increase tolerance of novel foods or to serve as a reminder to be a good friend when your child sees his sister chew those "squishy peas."

ACTIVITY 14

GETTING YOUR EYES USED TO FOOD

Our taste buds grow and change as we get older. New foods are a challenge to get used to. But the senses can help. This activity uses multiple exposures and the idea of letting new foods "live on the table" to help kids try new things.

DIRECTIONS

This activity requires that you find a food your child will not tolerate (or has not tried before) and introduce it slowly to her by providing the concept that the food gets to "live" on the table or on her plate, first introducing her to tolerating the sight of the food, then the feel, and then the taste of the food. You will want to determine a "go away" time for the food in the case that the child still can't tolerate the food. During this time period, the food may show up on the table, but the child does not have to put it on her plate or taste it.

Here's a script you can use with your child (note that instead of having the food be on the table for one day, you could keep it there for a week, then move it to the child's plate):

> Let's start with a green bean. The bean gets to live on the table today so you get used to its smell. Tomorrow, one bean begins to live on your plate–you don't have to eat it but your have to look at it with your eyes, to get your eyes used to it. Next, you have to touch it, eventually lick it, and finally take a small mouse bite (the tiniest bite of all) 12 times. Then, if you still hate the food, it can go away for a *whole* 6 months before you have to try again by having it on your plate. It may show up on the table, however, and that's OK.

ACTIVITY 14, *CONTINUED*

POWER UP!

Let your child be the one to select a food *everyone* has to let live on their plate, have 12 mouse bites of, and get used to. You can take turns as a family choosing the food. You might have to eat a sour gummy worm (yuck!) to incorporate her choices, but remember, you're working on increasing the well-being of the whole family!

ACTIVITY 15

TWO TRUTHS AND A LIE

Ask your child, "What happened at school today?" and you are most likely going to get "I don't know" or "Nothing" for a response. This game will encourage fun and sharing while helping each family member build understanding and insight into each other's days. In addition, developing the skills to differentiate between when a person is lying and when he is telling the truth requires us to listen carefully, read facial expressions, and use our own tone of voice to be "tricky." We include this game in the mealtime section because it's a good way to get the family sharing at the dinner or breakfast table.

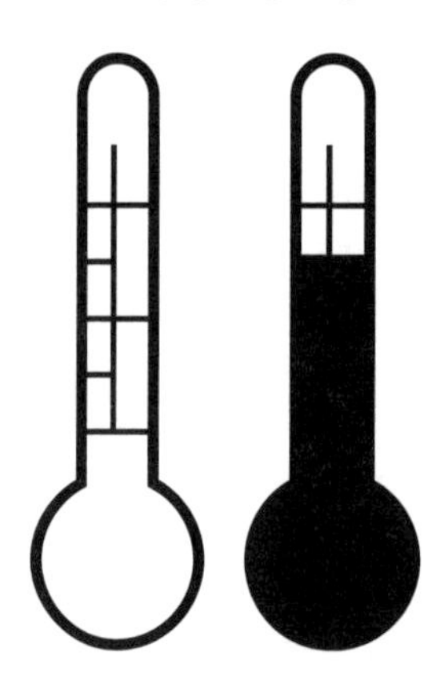

DIRECTIONS

Each player will write down two true things and one lie about him- or herself or his or her day on a piece of paper. (Alternatively, you can just think of them and not write them down, especially once kids get used to playing the game.) The lie should not be too obvious. Each player can share his or her three statements aloud to the group. Each player then guesses in turn which statement the player has fabricated. The lie is not revealed until everyone has guessed.

Here's an example from our dinner table:

> Today I lost a shoe when I was getting onto the bus and the driver had to stop for me, open the door, and let me get it back. I ate worms for lunch, and my teacher let us dance on the desks.
>
> Lie: I lost my shoe. I ate gummy worms at lunch, and today was Friday, when my teacher lets us have a dance party if we get all of our work done and we're packed up and ready to go 10 minutes before the bell rings!

ACTIVITY 15, *CONTINUED*

This activity can be adapted so that the child is given more support. Instead of having the child guess the lie by him- or herself, the group as a whole can come together to discuss what everyone thinks could be the lie. This will also help the child to hear other children and adults reasoning.

ACTIVITY 16

FAMILY MEALS SENSORY STYLE

You have heard of the importance of eating a rainbow and that we get used to how food looks (we call this "eat first with our eyes"). But food is a feast for the senses! How do you describe the taste of foods? Try it. If you or your child uses words like "juicy," you are describing tactile sensation. Smooth? That's tactile too. Crunchy? That's proprioception. The way you describe your favorites give you some clues about what sensory experiences you enjoy. Work with your child to find something for all seven senses! Can you do it? Think about the sensation of food. As you attempt the activities below, rank the experience with your child. Does she really enjoy visual foods? Circle the appropriate number of stars. Four out of five may mean it was a pretty enjoyable experience. On the other hand, a one out of five may not be such a great experience for your child.

ACTIVITY 16, *CONTINUED*

		Ratings
Visual	Colorful foods–consider an orange meal with carrots, orange flavored chicken, orange beets with spinach (okay, that adds green), and orange sherbet for dessert. Serve orange juice to drink, of course.	★ ★ ★ ★ ★
Activity Performed:		
Auditory	Add Pop Rocks candy to pudding, add music to the background of meals, and think about the sound foods makes inside your mouth as you are chewing. Granola bars make a lot of noise, as do potato chips or nuts.	★ ★ ★ ★ ★
Activity Performed:		
Gustatory	Consider recipes that are spicy, bitter, sweet, or sour or meals that have a combination.	★ ★ ★ ★ ★
Activity Performed:		
Olfactory	Taste and smell are intricately linked. Play a detective game: Tell your child, "Close your eyes. Can you tell what you're tasting? Now pinch your nose, and take a taste–can you tell what food you are tasting?"	★ ★ ★ ★ ★
Activity Performed:		
Tactile	What tactile sensation do you like? Warm? Cold? Hot? Smooth? Creamy? Make a chart. Is there a pattern in your family?	★ ★ ★ ★ ★
Activity Performed:		
Proprioception	Crunch! Your mouth is amazing–it's built for breaking food, shredding food, and moving food around in there along with tasting and recognizing foods. The joints and muscles of your mouth are strong–heavy work in the mouth (e.g., crunching, chewing) can be very helpful when we feel stressed or need a dose of something to get us organized. Make a list of proprioceptive foods and add them to your sensory diet food pyramid!	★ ★ ★ ★ ★
Activity Performed:		

ACTIVITY 17

SOCIAL RULES OF MEALTIME

Eating and mealtime is a great place to practice social rules. One way to practice social rules is to think about how they might be different if your child wasn't eating at home. Let your child visualize being in another setting, having his meal with other people. As a family, you can think about what foods you would have in this setting and what the rules for good manners would be. This is a great way to help your child begin to think about how rules change depending on context or the setting.

DIRECTIONS

Make a list of places to eat (e.g., grandparent's house, aunt and uncle's house, a friend's house, a favorite fast food place, a picnic in a park, on a space ship, in the cafeteria, in a bear's cave, in a fancy hotel, with an alien, with a favorite movie character). Cut out your list into strips, fold each so the place is not visible, and place them in a can or jar. Let your child select a setting. Then, as a family, talk about how the foods and rules might change in this setting.

POWER UP!

Turn this activity into a history lesson: How did people eat before they had flatware? How and what did the Romans eat? The Native Americans? How did Columbus and his men eat on a ship? Making mealtimes fun and interesting helps children associate food and eating with enjoyment, while adding socially rich opportunities helps them expand their habits and routines associated with the ritual of family meals.

ACTIVITY 18

GO FISHING

This activity targets the tactile system, as well as the oral motor system, as your child attempts to "fish" out candies from her dessert. It does require that you create the dessert before the activity, but we encourage you to let your child help with that task, as you'll see in the directions below.

DIRECTIONS

You will need graham crackers, Swedish fish or other gummy candies, blue gelatin, and whipped cream (optional) to make this dessert.

Place four graham crackers into a plastic bag and let your child use her hands to squeeze and crush up the crackers until they become "sand." In a large bowl, empty the bag of sand and place a few Swedish fish on the bottom. Follow the recipe for quickset on the box of gelatin. Use blue gelatin to fill the bowl, hiding the candy on the bottom, or allow the candy fish to "float" in the dessert by pouring in some gelatin, placing a few fish, and repeating this layering effect.

When it's time to serve the food, add a topping of whipped cream (for foamy waves). Let your child serve the gelatin dessert. This is particularly good for children revealing overresponsiveness to tactile input.

Have your child use her hands to retrieve the candy one piece at a time when she's eating it (not the best of manners, so perhaps not the dessert to serve at formal events, but in this activity, we're looking for tactile input).

Be sure your child likes the particular candy you've chosen for a motivation factor. If this is not a treat of choice, replace it with one that is more desirable.

ACTIVITY 18, *CONTINUED*

POWER UP!

This is a great dessert for birthday parties. Consider making individual cups using small clear plastic cups. Place a tablespoon of "sand" on the bottom of the cup, a few fish in each cup, and the blue gelatin on top. Top with whipped cream and sprinkle with blue sugar crystals! If your child can handle a bit of friendly competition, you can vary the number of fish in each cup (especially if you use white cups) and see who can "catch the most fish" or race to catch all of the fish.

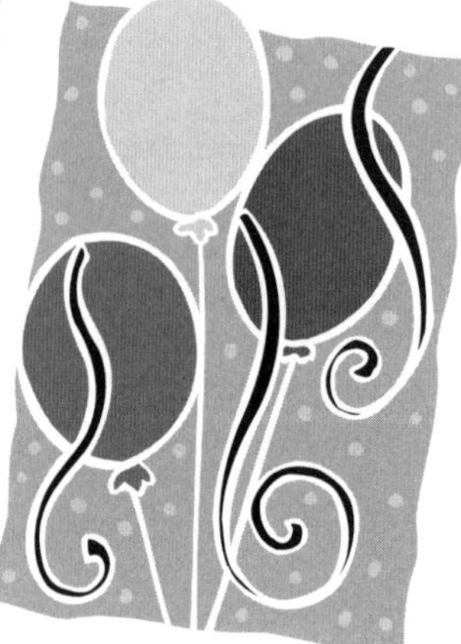

Chapter 6
School

School is one of the key areas of occupation for childhood, along with play and daily life skills. Getting dressed in the morning, picking out appropriate clothing, making it to the bus on time, doing homework, and studying for tests are all very important habits, routines, and rituals within the context of school and preparation for academic tasks. Sensory-based strategies can help a child be successful and ease the stress on the family.

Just as adults use calendars, grocery lists, and to-do lists to enhance memory, children also benefit from visual reminders. Visual and auditory reminders can be helpful sensory strategies for organization and time management. Any stimuli can be used as helpful reminders or deterrents.

Much like sleep, setting up the environment, using sensory strategies to support optimal focus, and establishing productive habits and routines are keys to academic success and reduced family stress related to homework and school-based occupations.

ACTIVITY 19

HAVE A PLACE TO THINK

A Thinking Cap Corner is a place for your child to do homework and/or study. This designated area should be designed to be comfortable, quiet, and with few distractions. Work with your child to create a space that has just the right chair, desk, and supports she needs.

For example, because sound can be very distracting to a child when she is trying to complete homework tasks, you may want to have earphones in the work area (some children need the extra sensation of sound, however, and you'll want to work with them to create an appropriate music selection for homework time). Think about all of the materials the child will need and create a small box that has all of the tools of success: a glue stick, sharp pencils, a good eraser, chewing gum, markers, and so on. Allow your child to help create her homework station (i.e., decorations, color of lamp, type of pencil box, notebooks, etc.) to increase her willingness to use this area for homework. Consider adding a white wipe-off board and make a list of what your child needs to accomplish, then mark the to-do's off the board as they are done.

POWER UP!

Consider the senses! Adult learners can concentrate for about 15 minutes before we need a break. We might have a drink of coffee or we will fidget or get up and go for a walk. Set a small timer and after 10–15 minutes, give your child the chance to wiggle. You can use the whiteboard to list out planned wiggle breaks, such as "Take one minute and get a cold drink" or "Take a 5 minute break and go outside for a quick walk" or "Listen to your music for 5 minutes," as to-do's in between homework tasks. Keep track of how long homework takes when you allow your child to take a break and when you don't.

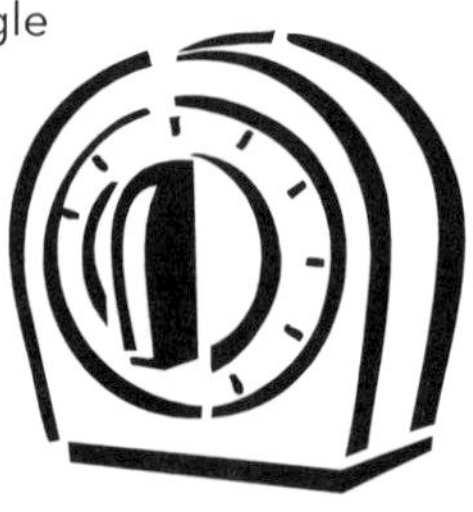

ACTIVITY 20

THE DROP-OFF ZONE

The Drop-Off Zone (some children may prefer to call this "jail") is a designated place in the home for children to leave their school things. Children who are disorganized benefit from having external organizational systems to help them compensate for the lack of internal organization. Having a designated place for items can help serve as a visual reminder and promote the development of organizational skills, but more importantly, can help a child *feel* more organized. For children who have sensory processing difficulties, bright colors may be needed to get their attention, so you may want to try colors as a strategy. For example, having bright red hooks near the door can serve as a reminder that this is where items for school are stored. Red means stop and pay attention and can cue kids that something important hangs there.

Parents can emphasize the importance of organizational skills when introducing the Drop-Off Zone. Think about having school-related materials like lunchboxes, coats, and backpacks all stored in one spot to alleviate stress in the morning. To use the "jail" theme, if you find the lunchbox on the floor in the kitchen, you call a "jail break" and ask your child to get that box back in jail! This adds a bit of levity to an otherwise annoying moment. You will have many opportunities to present the habit of using organization as a stress buster, so use praise liberally! For example, you might say, "Oh, Joe, look–your backpack is just where it should be and I didn't have to stress a minute over where to put this permission slip for your field trip! Good job buddy, that really helps Mom." Praising the child for his efforts helps teach the habit of putting each item related to school in its place.

POWER UP!

Once a week, set a timer and together, as a family, move through the house and find items that have escaped from their designated space. Return everything where it belongs. If your child gets done before the timer goes off, that's now her free time!

ACTIVITY 21

LEARNING MATH FACTS WITH JUMPS!

Physical activity and exercise can have an impact on cognitive skills, attitudes, and academic behaviors. Exercising while studying can boost a child's attention and improve her cognitive powers. Use this strategy particularly when your child needs to study factual information like naming the states, math facts, or spelling.

DIRECTIONS

Have the child stand in front of you and ask her, for example, to practice her times tables (say, 4 x 1 = 4, 4 x 2 = 8, and so on) while doing jumping jacks. For spelling, have the child spell the word first. If she can spell it correctly, no problem, you move on. If there's an error, write out the problem area, and increase attention to that part of the word through sensation. For example, if the child says, "F-E-B-U-R-A-R-Y," then write out "F-E-B-R-U-A-R-Y, being sure to show the child the error. Then, have the child do jumping jacks or clap while singing out the letters. When she gets to the "R U" that was previously missed, she should scream it out loud. For example, it might look like "f-e-b-R-U-a-r-y." This promotes memory, and it's so silly it can make learning more fun.

POWER UP!

Use a metronome to increase internal rhythm to the learning; for example, saying the multiplication tables to an 80 beats per minute metronome and then moving up to 100 beats per minute and so on can sometimes really help!

ACTIVITY 22

ACTIVITY CLOCK

Sensory overresponsivity can lead to feeling overwhelmed, anxious, and exhausted. Sensory underresponsivity can lead to feelings of depression and fatigue. Seeking sensation can sometimes get us into the state of getting too much and then we're overwhelmed. We need ways to take a break and check our bodies to see how we're feeling, but who's got the time?

DIRECTIONS

Help your child to estimate how much time different activities take so he can have a better sense of his time and effort. Take some time together to list out all that the child does during his day: sleep (10 hours), eat (2 hours), play (2 hours), homework (1 hour), and so on.

On a 1-hour clock face like the one provided in Appendix A, page 138, draw out how your child spends his time, coloring in the pie chart of the hours. You will likely be surprised about where the time goes, and you can discuss with your child how, as a family, you may want to change some of your habits so each of you has enough time for play and leisure.

Rethink how you use small amounts of extra time each day and learn to savor little pauses. Make a list of such pauses: Step outside and get a breath of fresh air, think of something you're grateful for and smile, stretch, dance, sing, or tell a joke.

POWER UP!

Consider a time-off vacation once a week: Set the timer for 15 minutes and encourage everyone in your family to do something he or she loves for the entire time! You can set rules like "nothing with electricity" or "something that grows your mind, your spirit, or your friendships."

ACTIVITY 23

CLEAN UP THE BACKYARD FOR MATH AND SPELLING

Who loves spelling homework? Your child will if you clean up the backyard while learning. Sucking and blowing through a straw as this activity is completed provides proprioceptive input to the brain and aids with optimal alertness for tasks. Adding a straw to a learning task can promote attention and provide a playful break to what can sometimes feel like a Sisyphean task.

DIRECTIONS

Using your child's list of spelling words, type each word largely in a new document, then print two copies. For each copy, cut each letter apart, so the word *siege* would become five squares of paper, times two (so 10 letters total). You can do this for multiple words. Now, mix all of the letters up, scatter them in the yard, and play the game! You call out "Siege!" and your child places the straw on the S and inhales, creating a vacuum and sucking the letter up to the end of the straw. She then carries the letter, attached to the straw, to a spot on the table, and drops it on the table, continuing until she makes the word. Meanwhile, you are helping her find the duplicate set of letters *or* you are trying to take various letters to your own side of the table, thus cleaning up the backyard. It also works if you have siblings or peers race to complete the words.

POWER UP!

You can also use this for math facts. Cut out numerals 0–9 along with symbols +, -, =, x, and so on, and scatter them in the yard. Race to clean up the yard; whoever has more "value" at the end of one minute wins.

This is also a good time to teach sportsmanship to your children. Have them practice being a good sport at the end of the game, where the winner *always* looks at the other player, extends her hand for a shake, and says "Good game." Remind your child: That way even if you lost the game, you won a good friend you can play with again.

ACTIVITY 24

FIELD TRIPS

Changes to routines are stressful, even fun changes. A field trip can be very exciting but can also set up a disaster for a child who has difficulty with emotions, motor planning and sequencing, and other sensory processing difficulties.

Recruit as many sensory supports as you can to set your child up for a great day: Think of sensation as a dose, just like an antibiotic—the effects wax and wane throughout the day. Help your child "power up" for the day in advance with these ideas:

- Pack a power lunch using the sensory diet pyramid.
- Select clothing with maximum comfort in mind (today may be the day for wearing a tight sports shirt or shorts under the school uniform for deep pressure).
- Tuck a small ball into your child's pocket to serve as something to squeeze when he feels stressed. Remind him of the rules for carrying this object (it's not to be played with or tossed around freely).
- Pack something for your child to chew on—beef jerky, popcorn, gummy worms, or other chewy or crunchy snacks. You may need to check with the school first and let them know you are bringing these food items, as some schools have rules about what can be brought by children on field trips.
- Prepare by visiting the site of the field trip with your child *prior* to the school trip; knowing what to expect can go a long way to helping your child feel organized and can help you strategize for what to pack.

POWER UP!

Create a story about the day and help your child prepare by talking through what to expect, what will be exciting, what might be stressful, and what he can do if he feels overwhelmed.

Chapter 7
Bedtime Routines

Regular schedules and bedtime rituals impact our ability to function at our best. Children with and without sensory disorders need to establish good sleep hygiene, and bedtime routines are essential ingredients. Routines should be a time for quality interactions—reading or telling a story, having reassuring chats, or having a routine snack or drink. Children with sensory processing difficulties have more frequent problems falling asleep and staying asleep throughout the night; they struggle with arousal and relaxation and as a result, bedtime is one of the most difficult times of the day for families with children who have trouble modulating their sensory system (Bagby et al., 2012; Schaaf et al., 2011).

You will want to speak with your doctor to rule out any sleep disorder such as sleep apnea or parasomnias—disorders of "partial arousal" that lead to unusual behaviors during sleep like sleepwalking or talking.

You can think about your child's environment, sensory system, and current routines to promote better sleep hygiene and to help your child relax at bedtime. Do an audit of the environment: Is the room too hot? Too cold? What about the bedding? Temperature regulation is part of the tactile system—if your child has difficulty processing tactile sensation, then she may also have difficulty regulating her temperature. Although you may need four blankets to sleep comfortably, your child may want a different temperature altogether! What about the textures of the bedding or the pajamas? Some can be very arousing—maybe your child wants his feet out or maybe he wants the sheets tucked tight? You will have to be a detective and work with your child to identify what feels just right. Does she like loose clothing? Tight? Furry pajamas or no pajamas at all? Are there noises in the environment that are alerting? Children with sensory processing difficulties often have trouble filtering out noises like a drip of water on the roof, Mom putting dishes into the dishwasher, or their brother's feet rubbing against his sheets. The visual system can also be challenged—new studies have shown the increase of streetlights has disturbed our sleep patterns and even the moon can interrupt the production of melatonin and affect sleep rhythms.

And don't forget, if your child is having trouble sleeping, chances are you aren't sleeping well either—nothing makes a parent crankier than lack of sleep! The airlines have it right—always put your oxygen mask on first so you can care for those around you.

Sensory strategies can help aid in calming a child when preparing for bed. Recall when your child was a newborn and you went to lie her down, on her back, in her bassinet. If she was wide awake, it was almost impossible for her to fall asleep. Therefore, you, like most parents, probably used a swaddle technique to simulate the comfort of the womb. As our children grow, things do not change too much. If you are having trouble getting your child to sleep, think about how you use deep pressure strategies—tucking your child in at night, fluffing the pillows so they provide just the right pressure to the head, putting on soothing music or sounds, having a special stuffed animal to hug, and drinking warm milk. You can intensify the strategies you are intuitively using and begin to gather additional sensory strategies, such as a visual strategy of making sure the child has

> Remember, deep pressure and temperature activate the touch system. A weighted blanket provides calming sensations by activating the deep pressure touch system and warm milk provides input to that same system to promote a calm, organized system. Spiced milk (for example, cinnamon) is an olfactory strategy and provides what is, to most people, a calming scent. You can experiment with what works for you and your child.

something soothing to look at or an olfactory strategy of using smells that are calming.

ACTIVITY 25

HAPPY HOUR AND LAST CALL

Happy hour is an adult tradition, helping us mark the time between work and rest. You can take advantage of this technique at bedtime. As part of the evening routine, create a "happy hour" designated to take time to get ready for tomorrow, moving many of those nagging little worries off your child's list. Set out clothes for tomorrow, pack tomorrow's lunch, and get all of the homework collected and into the backpack. All of those worries are now gone, and you're ready for the "last call" of nighttime routines.

Create a list of wind-down activities in your home. One hour before bedtime, begin the routine. Your child's list might look like this one:

1. Say good bye to the day:
   a. Last call for drinks and snacks.
   b. Last call for worries or anything needed for tomorrow.
   c. Reflect on the day and tell Mom or Dad one thing you are grateful for.

2. Say hello to the nighttime:
   a. Take your bath.
   b. Brush your teeth.
   c. Get your bed nice and cozy.
   d. Hop in bed.

3. Say hello to sleep:
   a. Have a chat with Mom or a story from Dad.
   b. Talk about what you are grateful for in your family or friends.
   c. Last call for any more worries. Tell Mom or Dad, they'll write them down for tomorrow.
   d. Put on some soothing music and go on a relaxation meditation.
   e. Close your eyes and listen as Mom and Dad remind your body it's time to rest and sleep.

ACTIVITY 25, *CONTINUED*

Here is a short meditation you can use to put your child to sleep:

Squeeze your toes, squeeze them tight!
Then take a breath and relax, little toes, relax.

Squeeze your feet, squeeze them tight!
Then take a breath and relax, little feet, relax.

Squeeze your knees, squeeze them tight!
Then take a breath and relax, little knees, relax.

Squeeze your legs, squeeze them tight!
Then take a breath and relax, little legs, relax.

Squeeze your bottom, squeeze it tight!
Then take a breath and relax, little bottom, relax.

Squeeze your back, squeeze it tight!
Then take a breath and relax, little back, relax.

Squeeze your tummy, squeeze it tight!
Then take a breath and relax, little tummy, relax.

Squeeze your chest, squeeze it tight!
Then take a breath and relax, little chest, relax.

Squeeze your fingers, squeeze them tight!
Then take a breath and relax, little fingers, relax.

Squeeze your elbows, squeeze them tight!
Then take a breath and relax, little elbows, relax.

Squeeze your shoulders, squeeze them tight!
Then take a breath and relax, little shoulders, relax.

Squeeze your neck, squeeze it tight! Then take a breath and relax, little neck, relax.

Squeeze your head, squeeze it tight! Then take a breath and relax, little head, relax.

Squeeze your ears, squeeze them tight! Then take a breath and relax, little ears, relax.

Squeeze your nose, squeeze it tight! Then take a breath and relax, little nose, relax.

ACTIVITY 25, *CONTINUED*

Squeeze your cheeks, squeeze them tight! Then take a breath and relax, little cheeks, relax.

Squeeze your mouth, squeeze it tight! Then take a breath and relax, little mouth, relax.

Squeeze your eyes, squeeze them tight! Then take a breath and relax, little eyes, relax.

(Kiss each eye closed.)

Purchase or create small (1/2-inch tall) worry dolls. You can use small plastic animals, rocks, or other items. If your child has a worry, he can tell the worry to the doll or toy and tuck it under his pillow. During the night, the doll carries the worry away for him so he can rest and sleep.

ACTIVITY 26

READY FOR DREAM LAND

When putting a child to bed, think about what you can do to make sure his sensory system is ready for sleep. Put on some soft and calming music (auditory), turn on a nightlight or a lava lamp (visual; you can find a 15-watt bulb at most stores), or give your child a massage or a back rub (proprioception/deep pressure touch) with scented massage oil (olfactory). The deep pressure of the massage also allows the body to come into a calming state. Check the temperature (tactile) and think about something for the mouth (a sip of water, warm milk if it's before he brushes his teeth).

Where the mouth and brushing teeth routine is concerned, don't forget that mint is very alerting! Have your child brush his teeth early enough that he can relax after, and try flavors other than mint like Tom's of Maine fennel or silly strawberry. The soft tone of reading a book will also help bring your child's energy levels down. You can also sing a soft song or tell a story (auditory).

POWER UP!

Depending on the needs of the child, you may want to add giving him his favorite stuffed animal or blanket to this routine. You can add calming input if the blanket is warmed in the dryer or the animal has a nice smell; for example, think about tucking a cotton ball scented with something wonderful under the bear's ribbon collar.

ACTIVITY 27

IPOD/WHITE NOISE

Use auditory input to help calm your child's sleep environment. Sometimes a room too quiet can bother a child or a sudden sound can startle her. White noise can provide a constant light sound, which filters out other noises in the environment. A small water fountain can be helpful for some children.

Consider creating a sleep playlist on your iPod–you can add stories or meditations, too. These can also help to block out intermittent noises that can be alerting to the child.

Remember: String instruments can be alerting, deeper tones are more calming and grounding. Fast-paced music is alerting, and slow rhythmic sounds are calming.

POWER UP!

Think about a treasure hunt for sounds: What sounds does your child find calming? The ocean? Waterfalls? Airplanes? Trains? The sound of lava or rain or even storms? Make a soundtrack and add that to the environment.

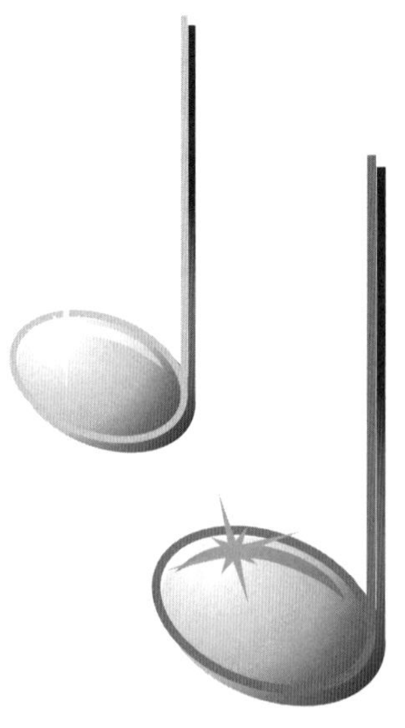

ACTIVITY 28

GOODNIGHT LIGHT! CALMING STRATEGIES FOR THE EYES AT BEDTIME

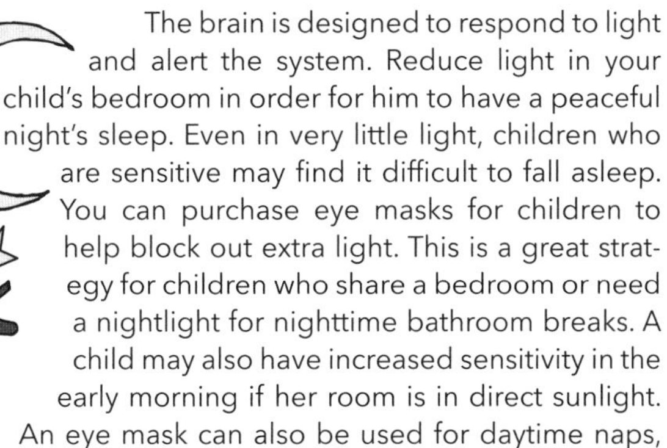

The brain is designed to respond to light and alert the system. Reduce light in your child's bedroom in order for him to have a peaceful night's sleep. Even in very little light, children who are sensitive may find it difficult to fall asleep. You can purchase eye masks for children to help block out extra light. This is a great strategy for children who share a bedroom or need a nightlight for nighttime bathroom breaks. A child may also have increased sensitivity in the early morning if her room is in direct sunlight. An eye mask can also be used for daytime naps, whether it is at home or in the car. If your child's room has a lot of windows or is located in an area of the house that is exposed to direct sunlight, purchasing "blackout shades" will keep the room dark at all times. During the day, you can simply raise them up to let in sunlight.

POWER UP!

Placing a string of rope lights or extra Christmas lights around a doorway will help to give a brighter light source that is still dim enough for sleeping. By stringing the lights around the molding of the door, the entrance/exit to the room is visible, allowing for a quick dash to the bathroom.

ACTIVITY 29

ANGEL SPRAY MAKES A MONSTER-FREE ZONE

At times, our brains send us false alarms—there are monsters under the bed, a boogeyman is hiding in the closet, there are gremlins behind the curtains. The sense of smell, olfaction, is a primitive system. The information for olfaction travels straight to the brain and interacts with the limbic system, the system of emotions. Children younger than 9 are still in the developmental stage of magical thinking—they still believe in fairies and angels and gremlins and goblins. We can take advantage of that development to help them at bedtime. This activity uses the sense of smell to help prepare the environment for good sleep.

DIRECTIONS

You will need a spray bottle of scented water such as rose water or a similar soothing smell. Create a label saying something like Angel Spray or Monster Be Gone. You can make a copy of the one in this book and cut it out for your bottle, too. Right before the lights go out, explain that you're going to spray the Angel Spray to keep the monsters away. Spray liberally around the room and then tuck your child in and say good night. You can also use a wall plug-in or air freshener that is only brought into the room at bedtime, giving your child's room a stimulating fragrance all hours of the night. In the morning, unplug or put away the air freshener so the smell will not be floating through the room all day. Providing constant stimuli to your child's brain will help to further develop his sense of smell.

Dr. Whitney & Dr. Gibbs'
Monster Be Gone Spray

ACTIVITY 29, *CONTINUED*

POWER UP!

Create a fun story–something about how monsters *hate* anything pleasant, like the scent of roses in the angel spray. Tell your child that when monsters smell it, they overreact (you can pretend to overreact to the imagined smell here) and run home to their mommies for something stinky.

ACTIVITY 30

SELF-ADMINISTERED MASSAGE

Deep pressure touch and input to the joints and muscles helps us feel calm and organized. Massage is a great strategy for helping children soothe themselves and sink into a relaxed state. A child responds better when he receives extra firm hugs, so why not do this all night long? Think about using spandex or jersey sheets or a sleeping bag or even a sleeping bag liner to keep your child tucked into a tight wrap for a great night sleep. To get the most out of the spandex sheets, secure the sheets under the mattress at the bottom and one side of the bed; after your child has crawled under the covers, tuck the last side of sheets under the mattress to create tension in the sheets. You can increase the deep pressure input by using a weighted blanket. A quilt is a heavy blanket that can be used as a substitute or two or three fleece throws work just as well. They will not weigh as much as an actual weighted blanket but they create the same sensation. You can also create your own sleep-sack or weighted blanket using the instructions in Appendix B, page 150.

> You can rent these items at a local outdoors store like REI for a few dollars; try them out at home before you invest in something.

POWER UP!

Deep pressure treatments before bed will help to give your child one last squeeze before he rests his eyes. Deep pressure treatments are tight hugs that last for about 10–15 seconds. Wrap your child in a blanket and sit him on your lap, then hold him tight. Cuddling your child during bedtime stories is a great way to not only bond with your child but also get in the last-minute body stimulation that he may need. Holding your child tight during story time is an easy way to achieve your goal.

ACTIVITY 31

COZY NEST

The muscle sense, or proprioception, tells us where our body is in space even when our eyes are closed. If this system is under-registering information, a child can feel out of sorts when she closes her eyes. Many children enjoy being in small places, like a tent, as such small spaces help them feel protected in a large world. Being in an enclosed space, like a bed full of pillows, will provide the touch children crave. Think about creating a "nest" for your child at night—provide a comfortable and safe space with your child's favorite texture for her to retreat to at bedtime. You can create this nest with one or two layers of pillows or blankets or by marking off space with chairs or other furniture. A small child-size indoor tent with your child's favorite pillows, blankets, and stuffed animals is a great enclosed sensory nest. Having a tighter, more confined space will allow your child to receive the sensory input she is craving.

A comfortable chair that has armrests will also work as a sensory nest. Placing pillows or blankets along each side of your child will make the chair "hug" your child. Using a chair will also give her a little more breathing room. It is a bigger, more open space that will still provide stimulation to your child.

POWER UP!

Make up a story about the nest—set up the space by adding favorite stuffed animals around the nest and let them "stand guard" all night. You can even hang a small battery operated lantern for a nightlight in the nest or tent area.

ACTIVITY 32

BATH TIME

Many parents struggle with bath time with their children. Children with sensory processing difficulties are more likely to have trouble with this activity because it is an enriched sensory environment with a lot of unexpected touch. Changing temperatures is also very alerting to the tactile nervous system and can feel very overwhelming for a child. This is a time for your child to unwind after his long day, begin to relax, and transition to bed. How can we make the dreaded bath more fun and less overwhelming? A few suggestions are provided in the chart on the next page.

ACTIVITY 32, *CONTINUED*

Sensitivity	Modification/Activity
Light	If it is safe, turn off the bathroom lights and fill the bathtub area with glow sticks. Children love glow sticks and filling the bathtub will illuminate the water. Leave the bathroom door open or keep a large flashlight on and close by to let in sufficient light. Remember, glow sticks can be a choking hazard so never leave a child unattended!
Touch	Check the temperature of the water; let your child test it first by sticking in a hand or foot before being submerged. Remember, what feels good to you may feel scorching or frigid to your child. Test out different textures for washcloths. A simple cotton washcloth may do the job but a loofah or sponge could work better for your child.
Smell	Shampoos, conditioners, and soaps could have varying scents that overwhelm your child. Taking a trip to the store to test out the items before purchasing them will help to eliminate any struggle from your child. If you cannot find a scent he likes, go for something fragrance-free.
Body	If your child is a wiggle-worm and you have a hard time getting her clean in the tub, turn it into a game. Play "Mommy Says," and when it's time to wash each body part, that is what she has to move. For example, "Mommy says raise your arms up high to the sky" is a great way to wash under your child's arms. Wall crayons or bath paints can be a little messy but will give just enough sensory input to keep your child busy long enough for a bath.
Vestibular	This system attends to changes in the position of the head, so putting your child's head back for shampooing can be very disturbing. Consider allowing your child to wear swim goggles to protect his eyes and having "rain" dump down on his head from a cup.
Sound	Water can sound pleasant or can remind us of getting splashed and being cold. Think about adding some soft music to the bathroom during bath time.

ACTIVITY 33

AUNT LORA'S FAIRY MILK

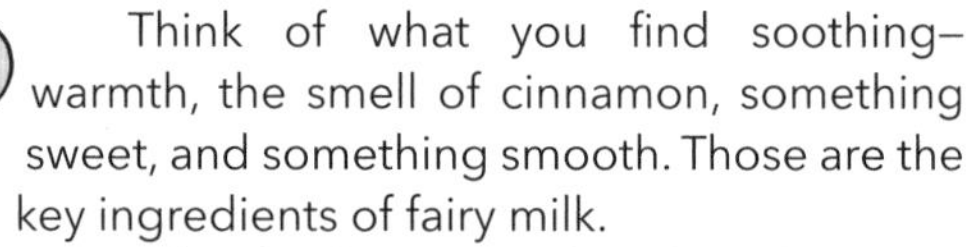

Think of what you find soothing–warmth, the smell of cinnamon, something sweet, and something smooth. Those are the key ingredients of fairy milk.

Before bed, or on nights when sleep just won't come, think about giving your child a nice cup of warm fairy milk.

> You can try hot cocoa, but be aware that chocolate contains caffeine and can be overly stimulating for an immature system!

DIRECTIONS

You'll need the following ingredients:

- 1/ 2 cup milk
- 1 teaspoon of sugar, honey, or agave sweetener
- cinnamon sugar or marshmallows (optional)

Warm the milk in the microwave for 30–60 seconds until it is lukewarm. Mix in the sweetener of choice. Top with a sprinkle of cinnamon sugar or a few tiny marshmallows.

POWER UP!

Add a straw to the fairy milk–sucking is very soothing and helps us get into a rhythm and calm our breathing. Tell a story about your family when you were growing up and what helped you feel cozy at night while your child sips his fairy milk.

Chapter 8
Holidays

We all use habits, routines, and rituals to help us feel organized and calm and to normalize our daily experience. The more internal disorganization we experience, the more we rely on external structure and organization to feel serene and at peace. Holidays are stressful because they bring change, disrupt routine, and demand new responses to the changing environment. As they come infrequently (once a year), we are in a constant state of stress as we attempt to adapt to the lack of routine. The contexts change and our homes are filled with new artifacts (e.g., indoor trees, fragile dishes, new smells, seasonal foods). For some children, especially those who struggle to feel organized internally due to delays in their sensory motor system, they can feel stressed and upset as the family attempts to enjoy the holiday experience.

Reflect for a minute how you feel when you are forced into an unfamiliar environment—there are many new and unfamiliar smells, sounds, and sights. Maybe you're in a new city and you have to navigate to a meeting, you have on new shoes or clothing you don't usually wear, and you're uncomfortable. You have coping strategies to help you modulate all of this novelty, but it's different when your child is in an unfamiliar environment or context during a holiday and the unfamiliar environment is her home. This can be very stressful. Unfamiliar environments may be overstimulating to your child—you have disrupted her internal state of equilibrium and she may express that feeling of being overly stimulated by displaying disrupted behaviors (Schaaf et al., 2011). Exposing the child gradually to the anticipated changes in routines when a holiday is approaching is a key strategy for preparing your child for successful transition to an upcoming special event, holiday, or new environment (Miller et al., 2007).

ACTIVITY 34

MORNING HUGS

This easy activity is beneficial to the child with hyposensitivity because it provides the child with deep pressure and proprioception. These sensory inputs will help to wake the child up to start his day! We include it in this section because it also helps prepare your child for the many hugs from loving family members to be expected during holidays.

DIRECTIONS

As you come into your child's room to wake him up, sit down on the bed and pat his back or stomach. As he rises, give your child lots of hugs. You can vary the intensity and type of hug you give as well.

POWER UP!

Practice! You can role-play and get ready for all of the hugs and touches your child might experience when traveling and greeting people. To think about out-of-town guests coming to stay, consider filling small toilet paper roll tubes with a short story and photo of relatives. Add a small treat. Open one a day and talk about your extended family member or friend; this can help expose your child to meeting new people and make the faces more familiar.

ACTIVITY 35

PLUG'EM UP EAR BUDS

If your child is bothered by noises while trying to do school work, noises on the school bus, or noise in the car, try this strategy to get ready for the loud roars that happen around holidays, the booms of the Fourth of July, the cheers at New Year's Eve, and so on! Wearing headphones can help minimize the sound and make your child more comfortable wherever she is.

POWER UP!

Earplugs can be more discreet than headphones. Depending on the need of the child, she can use headphones if the sound is too overwhelming or use earplugs to drown out some of the sound, minimizing the effect. Different colors and animal-shaped headphones are available; see http://www.autism-products.com for more information.

ACTIVITY 36

MUMMY WRAPS AT HALLOWEEN

Allowing your child to get deep pressure into his muscles and joints will get his body ready for uncomfortable clothes. You can use this throughout the year, but it's an especially handy trick around Halloween. Instead of overresponding to novel stimuli from those "weird-feeling" costumes, your child's sensory system will be prepared to tolerate (modulate) the sensation and his behavior will be better as a result.

DIRECTIONS

For this activity, you will want to get about 4 yards of spandex (dance costume material), a blanket, or even toilet paper. (The stretchier the material the better!) Wrap your child tight, coiling the material around his whole body—legs, torso, and arms. You can then have him chase you or try to break free of his bondage!

POWER UP!

Let your child wear a power suit under his mummy wrap! A spandex unitard, bike shorts, or spandex sports shirt can give consistent deep pressure and prevent the itchy/bothersome feel of the mummy wrap. This is also a great strategy for preventing the irritation from a Halloween costume, as it will serve as a barrier against the rough seams and novel material of most costumes. Giving the child comfortable textures against the skin can help make Halloween much more fun!

ACTIVITY 37

UNBAKED GINGERBREAD FRIENDS

Most of us enjoy making gingerbread for the holidays, but the real fun of the activity is cutting out the shapes! You can have the experience without the calories by using playdough instead of edible gingerbread. Adding sensation (e.g., smells, textures) to the holidays can improve acceptance of those novel feelings and attention to tasks.

For a child who seeks sensations, this gives her a way to practice baking for family and friends during the holidays and also gives her various sensory inputs, such as the texture and scent of the dough and flour, as well as hard work from rolling and cutting, which will give input into the muscles and joints. For a child who is sensitive, this promotes acceptance of sensation by exposure to the challenge.

DIRECTIONS

For this activity, you'll need the playdough recipe in Appendix B, page 155. You'll also need a rolling pin or canned good for rolling and cookie cutters for making shapes. Some forms of playdough can be baked so they harden—doing this could preserve the shapes your child makes. She can then decorate them, add a string (cut a hole in the top before baking), and turn them into ornaments or gifts.

POWER UP!

Think about making real gingerbread as a family and giving your final yummy treats as gifts (see Appendix B, p. 156 for a recipe). Children learn what is valuable (e.g., their time, their effort, their warm feelings) in a gift. If the child is too sensitive to the smell as it's cooking or being mixed, she can be responsible for other steps in the process (like bagging the cookies, making tags, or tying ribbons).

ACTIVITY 38

THE SHOPPING CART AS A TREATMENT STRATEGY

Shopping is often an opportunity for a meltdown, even for adults! What do you do to keep yourself functioning at the optimal level? Take frequent breaks? Have a snack? Pushing the cart is helpful too, although you may not have thought about that–the cart provides stability and proprioceptive input. You can provide this input for your child, too. Consider letting him push the cart, participate in a "treasure hunt" at the store to find certain items on your list, or be the "garbage man" who jumps on and off the cart to help retrieve all of the items you need. These playful strategies help your child use what's in the environment to modulate the incoming stimuli and help you get your shopping done.

Also consider allowing your child a snack in the store. Most grocery stores give samples. You can sample meats and cheeses at the deli counter and even if you don't have it on your list, they will often give a cute kid a slice of cheese. The deli workers almost always make it a sweet deal by smiling at your child and being very kind, and your child gets the opportunity to practice manners such as "thank you" and "please," even if he doesn't like the taste. Many stores will also have a "cookie club" in the bakery, a tray of cookies they offer to children as a sample. One store even had a "cookie club card" it gave to the children–it worked like a credit card (although they'd also give your child a cookie without the card), but it was a real pump to show that card and get a cookie! You can also make snack cups or baggies with dried finger food snacks like trail mix and crackers for your child to munch on while you're shopping.

DIRECTIONS

Pushing the shopping cart is the job of a responsible individual. You want to help your child understand that it is a privilege and comes with social rules. Explain that you can't run, you have to say "Excuse me" when going down an aisle, you can't play "crash cars"

ACTIVITY 38, *CONTINUED*

(but wouldn't that be fun?), and if you run over Mom's feet, you get a ticket. By pushing the shopping cart in the store, the child is receiving input into the muscles and joints of the body to help organize the child's environment and it helps him learn to attend to others in that environment. Selecting foods and putting them in the cart can be a way to pre-expose a child to novel foods he will be seeing during the holidays in the home. Setting up the story of a treasure hunt to find new foods for the holiday list can make this exciting to kids.

For the garbage man idea: You push the cart and your child stands on the side with his arm looped into the basket, hanging on while you push. When you arrive at the cake mix aisle, for example, you say, "Hop off and get me one of the red boxes of chocolate cake mix and put it into the cart *carefully*." This activity helps your child with visual scanning and listening to directions, and he gets good proprioceptive input into his body. Consider watching the video *Where the Garbage Goes* by George Woodard before trying this activity (he also has *Farm Country* and *Road Construction Ahead* videos; all are fantastic).

POWER UP!

You can create a punch card for your child to complete during your shopping trips. This can include things like saying "please" and "thank you," helping you with a good attitude, and pushing the cart without bumping anything (give two punches for this one). Once he reaches a set number of punches, he gets to pick one thing special to put into the cart, and you will buy it for him.

ACTIVITY 39

SCENTED TURKEY PRINTS

You are likely familiar with making turkey handprints for Thanksgiving, as most kids have done this at school or in daycare programs. You paint your child's hand with paint, she presses it onto paper, and you then decorate it with a pen to make it look like a turkey (adding eyes, legs, and the "gobbler"). This activity adds a little twist.

DIRECTIONS

For this activity, mix various spices such as cinnamon, nutmeg, or ginger into the paint. Consider allowing your child to smell the spices first and pick which one to use. Paint the child's hand and press the scented paint onto the construction paper.

If your child is overly sensitive and can't tolerate having her hand painted, try this:

1. She can paint your hand and help you press it to the paper and then sprinkle it with glitter and spices mixed together. When it dries, she can draw in the eyes and the feet and the gobbler.
2. You can cover her hand with plastic wrap or a plastic baggie and paint the plastic. Often a barrier will help the activity be tolerable.

It doesn't have to be Thanksgiving to make a handprint! Think about handprints for Christmas–paint the hands green, press the handprints in a circle, and make a wreath. Handprints for the Fourth of July can look like fireworks blazing in the sky if you sprinkle them with glitter, then cut them out, and tack them up on your wall! What about Mother's Day? You can make handprints and after they're dry, cut them out, paste them on popsicle sticks, and put them into a small terra cotta flowerpot for a "bouquet." Let your children have fun thinking of all the ways they can use handprints.

ACTIVITY 40

SCRUB-A-DUB SANTA BEARDS

Many children are afraid of Santa (and masks at Halloween) in part because he looks so odd with that big beard (or they wonder, "Where did Daddy go behind that mask?"). During bath time, your child can learn about transforming her image. Add bubbles to the bath (consider allowing your child to smell the scents at the store before you buy one, or get some unscented bubble bath; baby shampoo works well too). Whip up a good froth and let your child scoop it to her chin to make a nice foamy Santa beard. You can make fun Mohawk hair or pointy ears, too. Bring a mirror over so your child can witness his transformations.

POWER UP!

Put some soap on a sopping wet washcloth. On the *other* side of the washcloth (the one without soap), have the child press the cloth to her mouth and blow. A long train of bubbles will form and cascade down. Blowing is a form of deep breathing and can be very relaxing before bedtime!

ACTIVITY 41

STRESS BUSTERS!

Researchers have suggested that anxiety, stress, and being overresponsive to sensation are highly correlated: Many children who struggle to process sensory input are prone to feeling anxious. We all feel more anxious during holidays, but those of us who are *already* a bit more anxious can find ourselves feeling overwhelmed. Tantrums are common expressions of this overwhelmed feeling. Children show their anxiety by acting out, not following directions, or having a major meltdown right before bedtime. Adults show this anxiety by being less patient, making mistakes ("Did I *really* forget to put eggs in the bread?"), and having interruptions in our sleep patterns. The parent-child interactions can spiral downward and a pile-on effect ensues. Fortunately, there are many strategies that you can utilize to make this time less stressful. One often-used stress buster is yoga.

Consider incorporating yoga into your morning routine. Yoga will not only calm the body down for bedtime, it will also help to calm the mind and get us ready for a new day. Children especially enjoy the animal poses: cat stretch, downward dog, etc. You and your child can practice yoga together, getting your bodies calm and ready to enjoy the days/daze of the season.

DOWNWARD FACING DOG POSE

POWER UP!

Think about setting up a mindfulness room for your family—a cozy space with a few towels laid out will work. Light a candle for "time in" and blow it out when you leave to symbolize "all done." This space can be visited at any time you or your child need a calm moment. You can also think about bringing your pet into the yoga session for a boost to your calming Zen experience (see http://www.dogwoodtherapy.com/home.html for pointers).

ACTIVITY 42

COUNTDOWN SURPRISES

Anticipation is one of the hardest challenges for children. Being able to delay gratification and understand wait time are developmental skills that are expected to start around the age of 9. One way to help relieve the anticipation is to create a countdown calendar. Advent calendars are used by many cultures to help children count down or anticipate an upcoming holiday. We can borrow from that idea and create a tangible way to see the days "waning" as we look forward to a holiday. This example uses Christmas, but you can use this activity to count down to a birthday, the last day of school, or any holiday or event.

DIRECTIONS

First, figure out how many days are left until the event. If it's Christmas, there are 25 days from the beginning of December, so you will need 25 pieces of candy or a small treat. Think about the sensory system and select candy or a small toy that will provide deep pressure or input to the joints and muscles (e.g., taffy, gum, silly putty).

You can wrap each piece in tissue paper or just tie two pieces of candy together—end to end—with string or ribbon to make a chain. Each day, your child takes a piece off of the end of the chain. This is a fairly quick project—you'll spend most of the time tying the candy pieces together or wrapping the small gifts. You can hide small toys in tissue paper if you wish (parts of a small LEGO set, a small toy animal, or a ball are all good options) and add that to the countdown chain.

POWER UP!

Make a tree of ideas. Using the countdown idea, you can write out tags of fun activities that you will do with your child each day and hang them on a branch. Your child gets to "pick" an activity after he gets his chores done!

ACTIVITY 43

MORNING SURPRISES

Give your child an incentive for getting up and out of bed, and help her practice anticipation and surprise each morning. This is a quick and easy strategy to both provide sensory input to your child and ensure that everyone gets out of the house on time. Introducing morning surprises at nonholiday times of the year helps your child practice flexibility and dealing with changes to the morning routine—both things that happen often during holidays. This also works well if your child is staying in an unfamiliar home, or even just away from home, to help her feel comfortable coming to a new table in the morning or help her get dressed and ready for the day in a timely manner.

DIRECTIONS

Children enjoy making games out of ordinary things. Set the table for breakfast. Add a small gift or activity to your child's place: a small LEGO set, a pack of crayons, a MadLibs pad, a coloring sheet you downloaded from the Internet, or silly food (e.g., fun-shaped pancakes, colored milk). Think about the activities you receive when you go to a restaurant for some ideas.

Let your child know that as soon as she gets her clothes on, you have a surprise waiting for her at the table. The faster she gets to the table, the more time she will have to play with her surprise.

POWER UP!

Some children may not find this as exciting after the first few times. To spice things up, challenge your child to a race to the prize—whoever finishes first wins bragging rights for the day! We also advise using it more infrequently than some of the other strategies, so the child is never sure when the surprise might occur.

ACTIVITY 44

TALKING STICK

Taking turns in conversation, such as is often required at big holiday family meals and get-togethers, can be very challenging for children who have difficulty filtering sensation; who struggle with discriminating information through their eyes, ears, or body; or who are impulsive and have trouble regulating their emotions. We can learn about pacing, sequencing, and timing through our senses and can then match those internal sensations to the external rhythms in the environment. Many cultures use a talking stone or stick to better understand when it is an appropriate time to speak and when it is an appropriate time to stay quiet while listening to others speak. For example, the Native American talking stick is a traditional symbol that is used to keep order during meetings. This activity is beneficial during family meals or even family meetings to promote turn taking and participation. It is very helpful for children who are sensory seekers.

DIRECTIONS

Find a stick about 12 inches long and about 1 inch in diameter. Work as a family to decorate the stick–we used a strip of leather and tied some beads and feathers on, drawing from our family's heritage. Explain to your child that using a talking stick has two parts, speaking and listening–whoever is holding the stick has been granted time to speak. The other family members grant this power by listening and waiting. Whoever is in possession of the stick will be given respect and silence from the rest of the group in order to speak his or her mind. When the speaker finishes, he or she passes the stick to the next person who wishes to speak or places it back in the middle of the table. This gives children the opportunity to say whatever they like as well as learn essential listening skills. Use your talking stick during family meetings, mealtimes, or in the car.

ACTIVITY 44, *CONTINUED*

POWER UP!

Go on a nature walk together to find a stick, a piece of driftwood, or another item from nature along with objects of beauty such as an acorn (symbolizes growth), a feather (symbolizes flight and levity), and so on. Talk about what symbols represent your family and will be included on your talking stick. You can also discuss how the talking stick was used in Native American rituals or how Quakers use silence in their culture to develop the skill of listening to their own inner voice and the voice of wisdom in others.

ACTIVITY 45

PRACTICE HOLIDAY DINNERS

You don't need to wait for Easter to have colored eggs for breakfast or Memorial Day for s'mores! Sometimes it's fun to break up our routines and do something silly. For children who are anxious about change, frequent exposures to the smells, tastes, textures, visual experience, and sounds of food can reduce anxiety about those foods. Foods convey tradition and cultural values–why not have Christmas in July and serve Grandma's traditional morning casserole? Any day can be Thanksgiving with pumpkin pie or turkey. Researchers have found it takes 12 exposures of a food for a child to get used to it. Pick one food and set a goal to increase exposures and reduce behaviors associated with the novel food.

DIRECTIONS

Write out the names of several holidays you would like to practice on index cards or pieces of paper. Put the cards into a bag and let your child reach in and pull one out. Then, go about simulating that holiday–select the foods you would usually have in your family's celebration, decorate, dress up! Take some time to think together about your family's normal routine from morning until night and work together to contribute activities of the day and make suggestions about what to wear, what to do, and what to eat. Each time your child responds adaptively to a challenge, the nervous system grows and develops, creating greater resilience to change and higher potential for an adaptive response in the future!

POWER UP!

Make up a holiday with your kids. How about Kid's Day? Or Backward Day (the family could wear clothes backward and have dessert first)? Have your child help you think about the routines and rituals of this holiday, the foods, the decorations, and so on, then try it out and have fun!

Chapter 9

Social Participation

Families cannot create participation, but they can create spaces that enable and encourage participation in meaningful occupations and community opportunities. Beyond social skills, social participation has a positive influence on a child's health and well-being, and factors that affect participation within the environment, family, and child must command our attention when we create interventions and educational programs.

Social relationships are important at every age but especially important during childhood because playing together is the context in which children grow, learn, and develop habits of participation. During play, a child learns how to comfort another, to share, to cooperate, and to resolve conflicts. During social engagement, we learn how to make eye contact, to respond to questions, and to give compliments. Social participation is a broad concept referring to the opportunities we have to engage with others in satisfying social activities and events in many contexts—home, school, or the community (Cosbey, Johnston, & Dunn, 2010).

When thinking about social competency, think about whether or not your child accepts changes in routine, transitions when directed, plays appropriately with peers, or engages in nonadaptive behaviors such as tantrums. Can he use appropriate body language and personal space, follow attention when getting directions in a group (such as raising his hand), wait in line, listen during discussion activities, take turns, and wait his turn? Can your child stick with an activity until it is completed, stay calm after being upset, or keep control of his emotions? Can she recognize when she is at the "just right" state of alertness, try to solve problems occurring during social interactions, and make an effort to carry out problem-solving strategies? These are all prosocial behaviors and necessary for social participation.

The ability to modulate sensory input can greatly affect the degree to which a child will be able to successfully participate in social events. Family plays a pivotal role in supporting the child, helping her learn coping strategies and prosocial behaviors that will enable her to participate more fully beyond the family unit. When children have a developmental lag in the sensory motor system, they have a much narrower and less diverse social network than their peers, and participation is restricted to opportunities with close family members (Cosbey et al., 2010; Hilton, Graver, & LaVesser, 2007). Families provide a low-risk context in which a child can develop prosocial skills as well as the drive to engage in the community at large. Over- and understimulation can cause disruptions in social participation and overwhelm a family's coping mechanisms. Eliminating or limiting activities can cause a lack of social participation for the entire family. Play and social communication are two areas to target when parents want to improve social competency. Using sensation to support optimal play and social engagement is essential to the overall outcome of social participation.

ACTIVITY 46

COMPLIMENT BINGO

How do you teach someone to give a compliment? Helping your child think about the steps involved can be very helpful.

First, you have to attend to that other person with your eyes, your ears, your nose, and other senses. You may want to say you like the way her hair is fixed or the sound of his music or the smell of her perfume. We take in information from our environment with our senses and compliments are our responses to our sensory intake. Look at all of the ways your child can find something to compliment. You can ask him to be on a detective hunt with these simple questions:

- Did you catch someone in the family being a good friend?
- Using their eyes to find something?
- Getting their pajamas on?
- Doing their homework with a good attitude?
- Eating a good breakfast?
- Going to sleep nicely?
- Doing well in school?
- Exercising?
- Being creative?
- Being helpful?

Compliment Bingo is a game children can play, especially at dinner. Practice giving sensational compliments. Take turns telling each other something you like that you can see, then something that you can hear, taste, smell, or feel. See if you can fill up a card as a family and, if you can, you have improved your family's social well-being–you deserve a prize! Have a small prize available for the family–maybe having a play date after school at the park or family game night with another family from school. You can make your own BINGO card with what matters to your family using the many blank templates available online. We have also included a sample Sensory BINGO card in Appendix C, page 161 to get your ideas started.

ACTIVITY 46, *CONTINUED*

POWER UP!

See if you can practice random acts of compliments: Catch your family members complimenting each other at random times and that person gets a bonus. Maybe he or she gets to be in charge of picking what to have for dinner. Or he or she can pick out a game to play on family game night. Don't forget to catch Mom and Dad in the act, too!

ACTIVITY 47

TREASURE HUNT DINNER

We all like treasure hunts. This activity helps everyone participate in dinner. Think about a simple dinner (let's say you want to have tacos). You can hide the items your family will need throughout the house (salsa stuffed in a potted plant, a cooler hidden in the garage full of sour cream and cheese, corn chips or tortillas stuffed into the linen closet). Be creative–once all of the ingredients are found, you can work as a family to make a fun meal together!

POWER UP!

Invite another family over to share the hunt with you–a new form of potluck. You can write out clues that the kids have to decipher if your child is older. These kinds of hunts are especially fun when kids differ in ages, as the older ones have to help the little ones find the items you have hidden. Consider hiding items that will be found once it gets dark and kids need flashlights–small bags of toys like LEGOs can buy the adults a few more minutes of adult conversation time while the kids find and play with their "booty."

ACTIVITY 48

DON'T BE A SPACE INVADER!

Space invading happens when planets collide. Similarly, when a person invades another person's space, it can cause the "invaded" person to become upset and sometimes explode in anger. Ultimately, opportunities for future friendly encounters dissolve into nothingness if a child cannot respect another's space. You may never have taken the time to think about being a space invader, but children who are overresponsive to sensation are often hypervigilant about being invaded and find it very stressful. Children who are sensation seekers can be invaders and those who are underregistering information can sometimes invade another's space because they are just not aware of their own body. Space invaders grab, touch without permission, refuse to share, stand or sit too close, use unfriendly words and gestures (e.g., stick out their tongue), move all of their papers onto another child's side of the desk, or put their stinky shoes on a sibling's bed. Use your talking stick and have a chat at dinner to talk about space invaders in your family—make a list of any invaders and problem solve what you can do to turn them into friendly space beings.

POWER UP!

Use a tape measure and measure the space between family members, their chairs around the dinner table, their sides of the room, and so on and have a conversation at dinner about how much space you each need to feel like you have enough!

ACTIVITY 49

DETECTIVE AGENCY

To be a detective, your child will have to make guesses, pay attention to detail, plan her movements, anticipate consequences, and infer information from the environment using all of her senses in a purposeful way to solve the mystery. This fun game can be saved for Family Game Night or played any time.

DIRECTIONS

One family member leaves the room and, while he or she is gone, he or she must change one thing about him- or herself. When he or she returns to the room, the rest of the family has to be a detective and deduce what has changed.

Some ideas for changes include:

- unbutton a button,
- take off a sock,
- take off or put on shoes,
- change your hair,
- take off your glasses, or
- roll up your sleeves or a pants leg.

POWER UP!

Think of the other senses: Can you change something your family would hear (like your voice)? Or something they would smell (can you put on some perfume or rub your hands with lemon)?

ACTIVITY 50

HUMOR KITS

Humor is any interaction that results in an emotional experience of amusement, pleasure, or mirth, usually involving an element of surprise and resulting in smiling or laughter. Humor is a developmental process, with younger children enjoying peek-a-boo and knock-knock jokes and older children learning more sophisticated humor. Important aspects of typical development and humor appreciation include social development; understanding others' attitudes, intentions, and expectations; and the ability to be mentally flexible. Humor helps us a lot in our social interactions, as it helps us change our thinking patterns, helps us shift negative thoughts to positive ones, promotes mental flexibility and perspective, and ultimately enhances wellness and health as a result. Humorous interactions are some of the most effective at building and deepening friendships.

Work together as a family and talk about what you find funny. Do you enjoy physical humor like Jim Carrey's? Linguistic humor like Weird Al Yankovic's? Once you've decided what you find funny, build a humor kit. A humor kit should contain joke books and humorous cartoons, movies, or songs.

POWER UP!

Think about having a comedy night. Let the kids turn what you have collected in your humor kit into a comedy show—make a movie of their performance that you can enjoy again in the future!

ACTIVITY 51

SUCCESSFUL PLAY DATES

Having a friend and being able to play is one of the most under-appreciated activities in families with "typical" children. Those of us who have children with special needs know the angst of play dates and the longing for successful ones. Setting the stage for success is key–if social engagement is a challenge for your child, you can create a context for success with some planning and a thought toward the activities that will be organizing and supportive of interaction.

Before a friend arrives, identify three to five activities you will offer. When you or your child invites the friend over, make sure it is clear that you are inviting him or her over to specifically play these activities. For example, you could say, "I'm calling to see if Paul would like to come over this afternoon and build boats with Sam." You can have few alternatives set up that you have organized as a backup strategy. Set a start time ("I can pick Paul up at 3") and an end time ("and I will drop him off at your house at 5:30"). Limiting the time helps to create a successful experience. Talk with your child and identify any games or toys he doesn't want to share and put them away. Review any family rules with your child. For example, "When

ACTIVITY 51, *CONTINUED*

we fight over a toy, what happens?" Your child will then recall the rule: "It gets put away and neither of us can play with it." Review that part of a good play date is saying goodbye to your friend nicely. For example, "What do we do when it's time for Paul to go home?" "We say, 'Thank you for coming to play.'" "Do we cry and beg to play longer?" "No, we say thank you."

Organize the get-together for the children. Most children have difficulty in novel environments and a child with difficulties related to sensory processing is especially prone to feeling anxious in a new situation. You can use a therapeutic structure: First, get the body ready for good work (in this case the good work will be play); next, provide an activity; and third, offer a cool down to support transition. Tell both children, "We are going to have a cool drink with funny straws and then make boats. Paul, I'll take you home at 5:15." Let your child review the rules with the friend and show him or her where the bathroom is–you want the friend to be comfortable. Think about organizing the play date like this:

1. Welcome and orient to the family home/rules, open play (like LEGOs) to arrive to play without a lot of demands
2. Sensory strategy (e.g., cold drink, blowing through a straw, swinging, etc.)
3. Structured play activity (e.g., making boats)
4. Cool down (maybe a small crunchy snack or drawing or return to the LEGOs). Give a warning for time: "We have about 20 more minutes and then we'll grab our shoes and it will be time to take Paul home."
5. Give another warning when there are 10 minutes left: "Okay guys, you will want to finish up. You've made some great boats, let me take a picture of them so you won't forget them or, if you want, I can wrap one up for you to take home, Paul."
6. Time to go: "Okay, Paul, I have your boat and I'm taking it to the car, come on so you can show your Mom."

Select activities that are rich in sensory experiences to promote high engagement. Here are some ideas:

- Carve soap bars to make boats, add sails of cardboard, and sticks for masts. Float them in a small tub or kiddie pool filled with water.
- Make a tub of bubble solution and provide straws or other fun items to use to blow bubbles. Consider adding food

ACTIVITY 51, *CONTINUED*

coloring or allowing the kids to use their hands to make bubbles. Cover a small tube (like a toilet paper roll) with gauze, secure with a rubber band, and blow bubble foam.

- Gather sticks, nuts, and moss in the yard, and build a fairy house.
- Make cookies for a party.
- Hide small tokens or coins and have a treasure hunt.
- Dig a hole and fill it with water for toy boats or other bath/pool toys.
- Create a talking stick.
- Have a water balloon fight.

There are many other activities in this book to think about for your get-together.

POWER UP!

Transitioning after a play date is perhaps the most challenging. Think about a transition item. For example, taking the boat home to show Mom is a transition strategy. You can add a zipper bag with a bar of soap so the friend can show his parents how to carve the boat at home. This gets the friend thinking about the activity continuing at his home. This works both for your kid who has sensory challenges and your invited guest! Developmentally, most kids have trouble with transition until they're about 10 or 11–yours can be the house that other families have a good experience at, even when it's time to go!

ACTIVITY 52

KARATE BANANA

All of this work is making your child strong, right? Is she strong enough to karate chop a banana? Try this trick! Your child can practice humor on the family or with friends. Let her help you prepare some karate chop bananas for breakfast.

DIRECTIONS

You need the following materials:

- a banana,
- a toothpick, and
- humor and trickery.

When no one is looking, stick the toothpick in through the banana skin and "saw" back and forth, as if you are slicing the banana into invisible slices (you are). Continue this along the length of the banana, making multiple rings. Rub your finger down the skin of the banana; this will hide the holes you have made. The banana will appear undisturbed.

Innocently select the banana from a group and ask your child to give it a few air chops (chopping toward the banana in the air) and shout a magical incantation. Peel the banana, and "Eureka!"–slices will fall out of the skin!

Conclusion

Explaining Your Child

It is not always easy being a parent. Things can get especially challenging when we are having difficulty with our child's participation in everyday activities. To add to all of this, children with sensory processing disorders do not have a condition that is recognized or understood very well by others. Sometimes, the individuals we expect to have a good understanding do not. In fact, they may have a completely different perception of your child than you. What happens if your child's teacher has no idea how to get her to attend in class? Or, your parents are trying to convince you to allow your child to spend a week with them so they can "fix" his behavior? Even more concerning, what happens when your spouse thinks perhaps strict rules should be set in place and this sensory thing is not real? This leaves you in quite a position. How do you become the voice for your child?

As we stated at the start of the book, you are the expert. Perhaps you need to teach everyone else that sensory perceptions equate to human existence. Without sensory perceptions, life would not be. Heck, even plants require light to live. Every living thing utilizes some sort of sensory processing to survive. Therefore, your child's presentation of her self-regulation is essentially an action of survival.

She is trying to meet her needs through her actions. When those needs are not met, our behavior is affected. Not too many of us are happy campers when our needs are not met.

Anyone who has been on a recent airplane flight that took much longer to land than planned and runs out of snacks can relate. Perhaps this analogy can assist those nonbelievers to get a better idea. Even better, ask them how their bodies felt when they were on that plane. We would bet that upon exiting, they were moving as fast as they could to get off that plane! And when getting off the plane, they were probably not at their best cognitive thinking. The body was focusing too hard on fleeing and getting food and drink. At that moment, any demands placed on them probably would not be a good idea.

The above is just one example. However, the take-home story is that your child has what we all have, sensory needs. That is normal. The problem lies in our ability to be flexible in meeting others' sensory needs and understanding that our mismatches may be the actual source of the problem. When we all can better understand ourselves, our sensory needs, and how we establish our lives and environments based on them, perhaps we can better understand how a child who does not have much say in his schedule, activities, and contexts is affected. Ask those same individuals how they set up their offices, why they enjoy coffee in the morning, or why they use headphones on the subway. Why do they tap their foot when they are impatient or twirl their hair when nervous? Ask them how they would feel if those things were altered or taken away? Then tell them, "That is why my child is who she is! She has those same needs!" We all need to help children figure out who they are and provide those senses with stimulation. When we help the world around our children be more understanding and compassionate, we teach our child this: "Your gifts are for a reason. We will help you find ways to use your gifts to make the difference you came to this world to make." Some children have hypersensitive perception of sound—Rondalyn's older son had that and now he's a linguist and a polyglot; his well-tuned ears have served him well. The world indeed needs what our children can bring, even super-smelling, tasting, hearing, seeing, touching, and muscle power. We hope this book helps you enjoy your child and helps you and your family thrive as you engage in supportive routines within your family's day-to-day life.

Resources

Throughout the book, we've provided you with activities and ideas for your family to enjoy. In this section, we've included resources to help you easily implement many of the activities. Sometimes it's just easier to see something already in action than to imagine creating it from scratch!

Please feel free to share with us any ideas you come up with as you navigate through this book; we would love to hear from you. We've also added a few sites with extra activities for those weeks you may need more than one strategy to get you through.

ADDITIONAL SENSORY STRATEGIES AND INFORMATION

ATeachAbout.com—http://www.henryot.com/index.asp

FlyLady.net—http://www.flylady.net (This is a good resource for home organization tips.)

Living Sensationally—http://livingsensationally.blogspot.com

Making Sense of Sensory Behaviour—http://www.falkirk.gov.uk/services/social_work/children_and_family_services/support_for_children_affected_by_disabil/making_sense_of_sensory_behaviour.pdf

Native American Legends Traditional Talking Stick—http://www.firstpeople.us/FP-Html-Legends/TraditionalTalkingStick-Unknown.html
OT Exchange—http://www.otexchange.com
Sensory Focus Magazine—http://www.sensoryworld.com/SensoryFocus.aspx

COUNTING DOWN TO EVENTS AND HOLIDAYS

Best Advent Calendars—http://www.parents.com/holiday/christmas/crafts/best-advent-calendars/#page=1
Christmas Candy Countdown—http://www.craftster.org/forum/index.php?topic=417392.0#ixzz2UxwOsVhM

PROVIDERS FOR SENSORY TOYS

Pocket Full of Therapy—http://pfot.com
School Specialty—https://store.schoolspecialty.com/OA_HTML/ibeCCtpSctDspRte.jsp?sname=Special+Needs&rootSection=95750§ion=95750&minisite=10206
Southpaw Enterprises—http://www.southpawenterprises.com
Therapy Shoppe—http://www.therapyshoppe.com

MEALTIMES

Culture and Rituals of Eating—https://www.youtube.com/watch?v=HyVPfFKp7SI
Dysphagia Fact Sheet—http://www.aota.org/~/media/Corporate/Files/AboutOT/Professionals/WhatIsOT/PA/Facts/Dysphagia%20fact%20sheet.ashx
Puzzlemaker—http://www.discoveryeducation.com/free-puzzlemaker/?CFID=355277&CFTOKEN=12766806 (This is a great resource for making puzzles to have on the table during mealtimes.)

References

American Occupational Therapy Association. (2008). Occupational therapy practice framework: Domain and process (2nd ed.). *American Journal of Occupational Theraphy, 62,* 625–683.

Ayres, A. J. (1972). *Sensory integration and learning disorders.* Los Angeles, CA: Western Psychological Services.

Bagby, M. S., Dickie, V. A., & Baranek, G. T. (2012). How sensory experiences of children with and without autism affect family occupations. *American Journal of Occupational Therapy, 66,* 78–86.

Ben-Sasson, A., Carter, A. S., & Briggs-Gowan, M. (2009). Prevalence and correlates of sensory over-responsivity from infancy to elementary school. *Journal of Abnormal Child Psychology, 37,* 705–716.

Cosbey, J., Johnston, S. S., & Dunn, M. L. (2010). Sensory processing disorders and social participation. *American Journal of Occupational Therapy, 64,* 462–473.

Crespo, C., Kielpikowski, M., Pryor, J., & Jose, P. E. (2011). Family rituals in New Zealand families: Links to family cohesion and adolescents' well-being. *Journal of Family Psychology, 25,* 184–193.

Dengel, J. (n.d.). *Family rituals and traditions.* Retrieved from http://family.go.com/parenting/pkg-school-age/article-796126-family-rituals-and-traditions-t

Dunn, W. (1997). The impact of sensory processing abilities on the daily lives of young children and their families: A conceptual model. *Infants and Young Children, 9*(4), 23–35.

Dunn, W. (2001). The sensations of everyday life: Empirical, theoretical, and pragmatic considerations. *American Journal of Occupational Therapy, 55,* 608–620.

Foss-Feig, J. H., Heacock, J. L., & Cascio, C. J. (2012). Tactile responsiveness patterns and their association with core features in autism spectrum disorders. *Research in Autism Spectrum Disorders, 6,* 337–344.

Freedman, B., & Whitney, R. (2011, Summer). Strengthening family quality of life: A plan for your family's success. *SI Focus,* 8–15.

Green, S. A., & Ben-Sasson, A. (2010). Anxiety disorders and sensory over-responsivity in children with autism spectrum disorders: Is there a causal relationship? *Journal of Autism and Developmental Disorders, 40,* 1495–1504.

Hilton, C., Graver, K., & LaVesser, P. (2007). Relationship between social competence and sensory processing in children with high functioning autism spectrum disorders. *Research in Autism Spectrum Disorders, 1,* 164–173.

Mazurek, M., Vasa, R., Kalb, L., Kanne, S., Rosenberg, D., Keefer, A., & Lowery, L. (2013). Anxiety, sensory over-responsivity, and gastrointestinal problems in children with autism spectrum disorders. *Journal of Abnormal Child Psychology, 41,* 165–176.

Miller, L. J., Anzalone, M. E., Lane, S. J., Cermak, S. A., & Osten, E. T. (2007). Concept evolution in sensory integration: A proposed nosology for diagnosis. *American Journal of Occupational Therapy, 61,* 135–141.

Parham, L. D., Roley, S. S., May-Benson, T. A., Koomar, J., Brett-Green, B., Burke, J. P., . . . Schaaf, R. C. (2011). Development of a fidelity measure for research on the effectiveness of the Ayres sensory integration intervention. *American Journal of Occupational Therapy, 65,* 133–142.

Pólya, G. (1957). *How to solve it.* Garden City, NY: Doubleday.

Schaaf, R. C., Benevides, T. W., Imperatore, E., Brett-Green, B. A., Burke, J. J., Cohn, E. S., . . . Schoen, S. A. (2010). Parasympathetic functions in children with sensory processing disorder. *Frontiers of Integrative Neuroscience, 4*(4), 1–11. doi:10.3389/fnint.2010.00004

Schaaf, R. C., Toth-Cohen, S., Johnson, S. L., Outten, G., & Benevides, T. W. (2011). The everyday routines of families of children with autism: Examining the impact of sensory processing difficulties on the family. *Autism, 15,* 373–389.

Seligman, M. (2004). *Authentic happiness: Using the new positive psychology to realize your potential for lasting fulfillment.* New York, NY: Simon & Schuster.

Suarez, M. A., Nelson, N. W., & Curtis, A. B. (2012). Associations of physiological factors, age, and sensory over-responsivity with food selectivity in children with autism spectrum disorders. *The Open Journal of Occupational Therapy, 1*(1). Retrieved from http://scholarworks.wmich.edu/ojot/vol1/iss1/2

Whitney, R. (2012, February). Autism and family quality of life. *OT Practice, 17*(2), 11–15.

Appendix A

Reproducible Forms and Worksheets for a Sensational Family Life

SAMPLE CHORES CHART

	Daily One-Minute Chores	Child	Family Well-Being
Sunday	Put away seven escaped toys Wipe off bathroom sinks	Alex Zac	Help prepare one food for our dinner
Monday	Dust great room table Put away five escaped books	Alex Zac	Take out the trash
Tuesday	Dust living room tables Wipe off place mats on dining room table	Alex Zac	Sort recycling
Wednesday	Put away any escaped homework supplies Clean bathroom mirrors	Alex Zac	Put dishes in dishwasher
Thursday	Choice Chores!	All	Swiffer the kitchen floor
Friday	Put away escaped shoes Take dirty duds (laundry) to basement	Alex Zac	Sneak and do someone else's chore before they can (if you don't get caught, you get a treat)
Saturday	Strip sheets 27 Fling Boogie	All	Put lunch snacks into snack bags
Net	**Parents remove 15 minutes of cleaning!**		**Family add 22 units of well-being**

BLANK SAMPLE CHORES CHART

	Daily One-Minute Chores	Child	Family Well-Being
Sunday			
Monday			
Tuesday			
Wednesday			
Thursday			
Friday			
Saturday			
Net			

ACTIVITY CLOCK

Take an average day in your life. Think about how you spend each minute of your day. For example, how much time do you spend on sleep? Eating? Preparing meals? Studying? Work? Child care? Self-care? Write it all down. Using a 24-hour clock, determine the number of minutes you spend and shade the clock accordingly. Talk about your clock with your family and work together to change any expense of time that you would like to spend differently. Have each family member make his or her own clock based on his or her own daily activities.

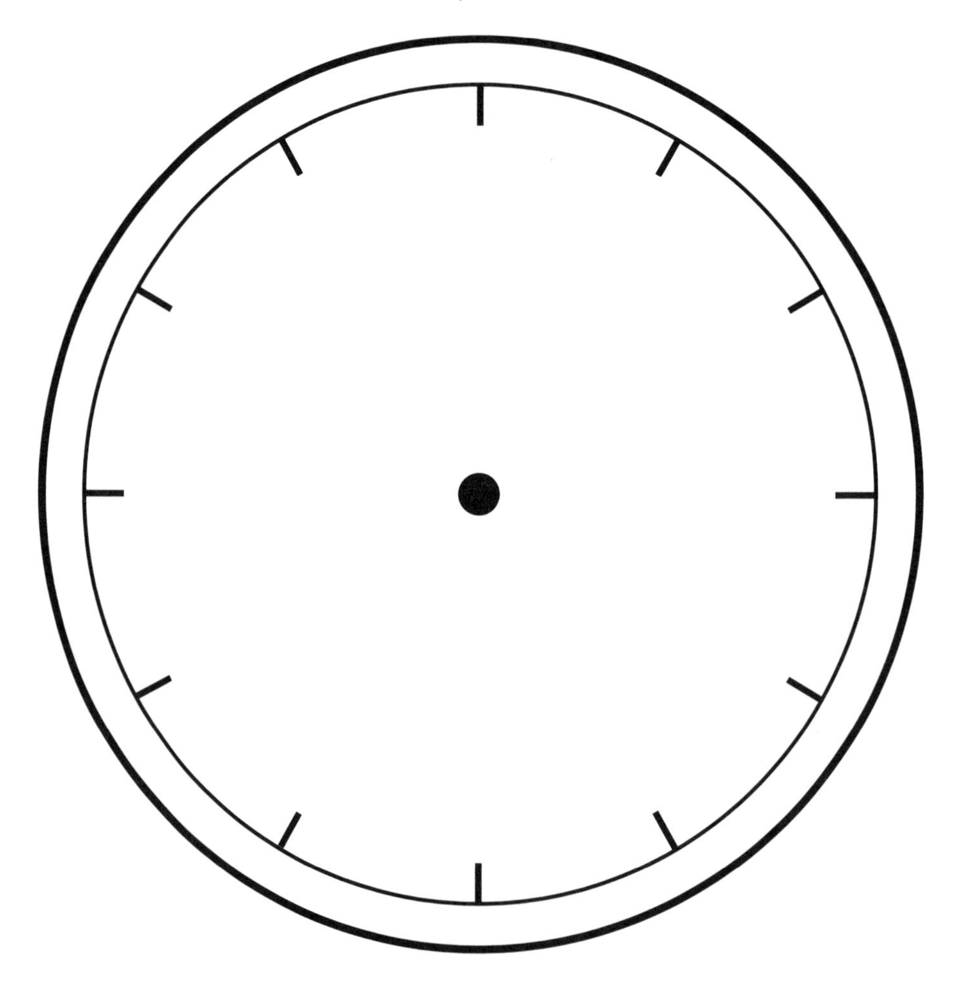

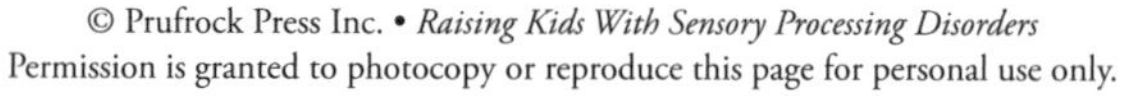

SENSORY DIET MAP

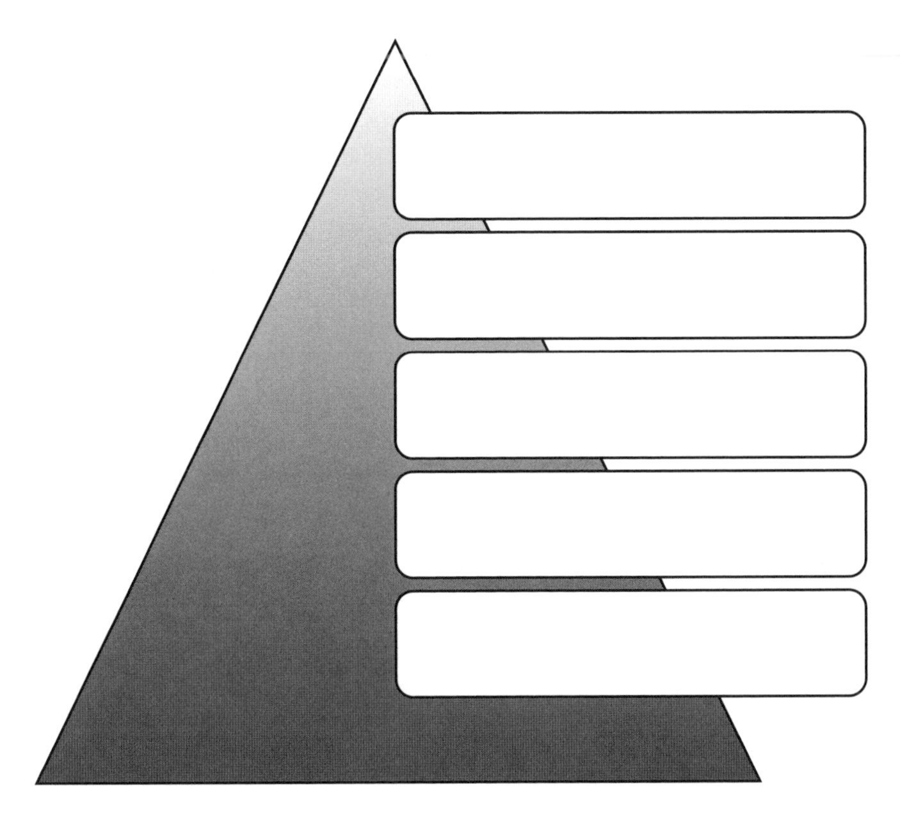

MEAL PLANNING CHART

Involve your family in planning meals, but keep in mind the sensory diet you have created for your child!

Day of the Week							
Breakfast							
Snack							
Lunch							
Dinner							

BLANK ACTIVITY DIARY

Child: ______________________ **Date:** ______________________

Activity	**Time** *(When Was the Activity Performed?)*	**Duration** *(For How Long Was It Performed?)*	**Arousal Level Prior to Input** *(High, Low, Calm, Alert)*	**Change in Reaction?** *(Yes or No)*
Vestibular				
Proprioception/Oral Motor				
Tactile				
Visual				
Auditory				

EVALUATE PROGRESS: FORM

Problem Identified/Strategy	Goal/ Start Date	Midway Checkpoint Date	How Will You Know You Have Solved the Problem?	Date Goal Met

WISE APPROACH TO PROBLEM SOLVING

A SEMISTRUCTURED INTERVIEW FOR PARENTS

What are the problems you are experiencing with your child?

___

___

What time of day are the challenges more disruptive?

___

___

What activities seem to make things worse? Can you see a pattern?

___

___

What activities seem to help? Can you see a pattern?

___

___

What activity would you like to try? How will you know if it has helped your family?

___

___

Make a plan: Write the activity name, the page number, and your timeline.

___

___

BACK IN CONTROL SHEET

How do you feel?

Ask yourself: What does your body need so you can be ready for good work?

Good job! What worked to help you get your body ready for good work?

- Snack
- Listening to music/computer time
- Exercise/moving my body
- Playing a game
- Meditating
- Something else: ______________________________

Now I feel proud of myself!

MORNING ROUTINE: SAMPLE

What I need to do:
Get dressed, eat breakfast, and brush my teeth.

What my body needs to get ready for my best work:

- Magic Carpet Ride
- Cold milk with a straw

My checklist:

1. Get my underwear, shorts, and shirt on.
2. Roll over onto the carpet.
3. Get a ride to the kitchen.
4. Eat my cereal.
5. Brush my teeth.
6. Give Mom a high five.
7. Watch a cartoon if I'm ready in time!

How this helps my family:
Mom gets to have her breakfast.

How this helps me:
I have time to play on the playground at school when she drops me off.

MORNING ROUTINE: BLANK CHART

What I need to do:

____

____

____

What my body needs to get ready for my best work:

____

____

____

My checklist:

____

____

____

____

____

How this helps my family:

____

____

____

How this helps me:

____

____

EVENING ROUTINE: SAMPLE

What I need to do:
Pack my backpack for tomorrow.

What my body needs to get ready for my best work:

- Cold snack (frozen grapes).

My checklist:

1. Put my homework in the folder and put it in my backpack.
2. Pack my lunch and put it into the fridge.
3. Put on my pajamas.
4. Brush my teeth.
5. Get in bed when asked the first time.

How this helps my family:
The mornings are not as crazy when I'm ready!

How this helps me:
Dad has more time to read to me—we're finishing *Peter and the Starcatchers* tonight!

EVENING ROUTINE: BLANK CHART

What I need to do:

What my body needs to get ready for my best work:

My checklist:

How this helps my family:

How this helps me:

Appendix B

Supplies for a Sensational Family

WEIGHTED BLANKET

MATERIALS

- 2 yards of a top fabric
- 2 yards of a bottom fabric
    - Allow your child to choose his or her favorite color, design, or material.
    - Cotton is the lightest and most breathable fabric.
- Thread
- Poly pellets (used to fill a doll or stuffed animal and can be found at a craft store)
    - The weight you decide on will determine how much needs to be purchased.
    - To determine the weight, take 1/10 of your child's weight and add 1. For example, if your child is 50 lbs., you would want a 6 lb. blanket.

DIRECTIONS

- Place the right sides of the materials together, begin sewing 1 inch from the top edge, and sew three sides of the fabric together. Turn the blanket so the right sides are now out and the seams are hidden.
- From the bottom of the material, sew a vertical line or channel, every 4 inches, up to 1 inch away from the top of the material.
- Fill channels with pellets.
- Fold top edges in and stitch across.
- If you wish to make an extra pocket for the pellets, you can turn the blanket and sew horizontally to create small squares to hold the pellets. Push the pellets to the side as you sew each horizontal seam. We would recommend doing the top hem first or folding in and pinning your top edges together so your pellets do not escape while you're manipulating the material. Or only fill each channel a little at a time, sew across horizontally to trap those pellets, then add more pellets on top of the new seam, repeating until you get to the top.

WEIGHTED CAPE

MATERIALS

- 1 yard of fleece, flannel, or other soft material
- 6–10 small washers (found in the hardware section at the hardware store)
- 3–4 feet of 1/2-inch sturdy ribbon (grosgrain works well)
- Yardstick or long craft ruler
- Scissors or rotary cutter
- Cutting mat or flat surface
- Fabric marker/pen
- Thread
- Iron and ironing board

DIRECTIONS

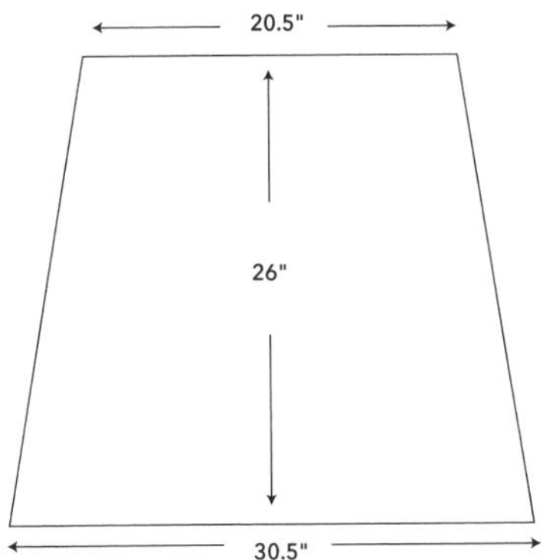

Cut your material using the measurements in the diagram. The easiest way to do this is to use a long yardstick or craft ruler and a fabric marker on a flat surface (like a cutting mat) and use a rotary cutter or sharp scissors. Mark each horizontal measurement, measuring the 30.5 inches on the bottom of your yard first. Mark each end of the measurement. Then, from each end of that measurement, measure 26 inches up from the bottom and mark lightly. Come in 5 inches on each side and mark those two end spots, drawing a line between them to make your 20.5-inch top edge. Using your ruler as a straight edge, draw a line from the top end spots down to the 30.5 measurement end spots and cut along your lines.

Then, hem each diagonal side with a simple 1/4- or 1/2-inch hem, folding the material to the back side, pressing it with a hot iron, then adding a top stitch to hold the hem in place. You can double this hem if you like for sturdiness, folding in twice instead of once. You will then need to create a casing along the top edge (20.5-inch edge). To create a casing, fold the top edge over by a 1/2 inch, press with a hot iron, and sew a top stitch along the unfinished edge of the fold. Thread the ribbon through this casing, bunching in the middle to make the gathered top edge of the cape. Secure on each side by knotting the ribbon. This will create an adjustable tie that can go around the neck. Now glue or sew the washers in even spaces along the bottom of the cape (the 30.5-inch measurement). Once this is done, fold the bottom edge in by 1/4 inch and press. Fold it in again so the folded edge comes up and over the weights. Sew along the top of this new hem edge. You may want to sew along this twice or use a zigzag stitch on top of your straight stitch for extra support.

Now you have a weighted cape—think about adding a symbol for power—W for Wonder Boy, Z for Zip Girl . . . whatever your child favors. We lived with Purple Man for several years. You may want to consider adding the symbol before adding the weights to make it easier to work with the fabric while appliqueing. Or, let your child help you pick out an iron-on transfer or use fabric paint to create his unique symbol!

WEIGHTED ANIMALS

Need some extra help for mealtimes or times when a little calm and sanity would be helpful? Maybe toilet training is scary and your child needs a heavy friend to help her feel more secure? You may want to make a weighted animal.

MATERIALS

- A stuffed animal
- 3 pounds of fish gravel
- Needle and thread
- Scissors

This works with any stuffed animal but can be especially good for a favorite friend. When no one is looking (this is important, as some kids can't stand to see their friends cut open!), find the seam of the critter and slice open a surgical seam of about 6 inches. Shove in a cup or two of the gravel. Large animals can take more weight.

Repair your incision with a whip stitch (look online for a tutorial if you need help with this stitch). Now you have a new friend in your bag of tricks.

Goodwill and other thrift stores often have a lot of stuffed animals for sale, pretty cheap! You can make one for everyone in your family or even one for each peer in your child's classroom.

CATERPILLAR TUNNEL/SLEEP SACK

Crawling and pushing against resistance helps to build good strong muscles and provides deep pressure input to the system.

MATERIALS

- 3–5 yards of stretchy material (spandex/dance costume material, jersey knit, etc.)
- Thread
- Pins

DIRECTIONS

1. Fold the material in half, hot dog style.
2. Put right sides together and pin the material along the sides.
3. You will sew a seam about 1/2 inch from the edges.
4. Turn the material right side out and you now have a long tube.
5. Have your child crawl through the tunnel.
6. Hold one end and pull back the excess fabric as your child crawls through to the other end; this way you can make the tunnel as long or as short as your child would like!

PLAYDOUGH

MATERIALS

- 1 cup flour
- 1/2 cup salt
- 2 tsp. cream of tartar
- 2 tbsp. vegetable oil
- 1 cup water
- Spices (ginger, nutmeg, cinnamon, cloves; optional)

DIRECTIONS

Mix the ingredients in a saucepan. Cook on low, stirring often until it forms a dough. If you'd like, you can knead in glitter. Use cookie cutters to cut out your family of gingerbread people. Decorate with sequins, buttons, and other fun materials you have around the house.

Instead of the spices (that make play gingerbread), you can add 1 teaspoon vanilla or other flavoring extract (e.g., orange, almond, strawberry, etc.) or add 1/4 cup of cocoa powder or food coloring. Experiment with touch sensation (e.g., texture from glitter, small toy animals) or other scents (e.g., grape, a package of KoolAid).

AUTHENTIC HOLIDAY GINGERBREAD

MATERIALS

- 1 1/2 cups of dark molasses
- 1 cup of packed brown sugar
- 2/3 cup cold water
- 1/3 cup shortening
- 7 cups all-purpose flour
- 2 teaspoons baking soda
- 1 teaspoon salt
- 1 teaspoon ground allspice
- 1 teaspoon ground cloves
- 2 teaspoons of ground ginger
- 1 teaspoon of ground cinnamon
- Baking sheet
- Rolling pin
- Cookie cutters

DIRECTIONS

Preheat the oven to 350 degrees Fahrenheit.

Mix the wet ingredients together in a mixing bowl using your hands (molasses, brown sugar, water, and shortening), then add the dry ingredients and mix. Let the dough sit in the refrigerator for 2 hours to get nice and cold. Using a rolling pin, let your child roll out the dough (if possible to 1/4-inch thickness) and use cookie cutters to cut out the shapes of your child's choice.

Put on a greased cookie pan and bake in the oven for 10–12 minutes.

POST OFFICE

Use lick-and-stick stamps to make mosaics. You can have your child make a design of his choice. Or you can make a specific design. Have your child make a rocket ship, house, or racecar with the lick-and-stick stamps.

This activity is a great oral motor activity as it can provide stimulation to the mouth. Because of the connection with the back of the tongue, it can be very calming. The posterior aspect of the tongue has connections with our nervous system involved in regulation. Another benefit is preparing the mouth for eating, specifically with our picky eaters. For our children seeking input to their mouths, this activity may meet their needs.

Appendix C

Additional Activities for Sensational Families

BINGO

BINGO is a game that has stood the test of time. Utilize this fun BINGO card to have your child take part in identifying his sensory experiences. Hang it on the fridge and use magnets as the BINGO chips. Throughout the week, your child will place a magnet over the activities performed. For example, a picture of a girl sleeping may indicate having a good night's sleep. The magnifying glass could representing "using your eyes" to find shoes in the morning without asking Dad to help or paying attention at school. You can use images that have meaning specifically relating to your child's needs. Use this as a start, but perhaps make your own with photos from your own family or drawings you and your child make together.

SAMPLE BINGO CARD

DECISION DOLLARS

When you catch someone in the family making a good decision, you can give them a note! Think about, as a family, what you will do with your earned decision dollars—can you have a dessert-first day? Buy a day off from chores? Good decisions build real energy in a family, and a decision dollar allows you to show that to your child.

SUSHI ROLL

Your child will make a sushi roll consisting of himself and items from his environment. In the morning, place his pants on one side of the room and his shirt on the opposite side of the room. Continue to place his clothing items and shoes on each side of the room. Lay a blanket down in the center of the floor. Have your child lie on one edge of the blanket and roll himself inside. Once he arrives at the other side of the room, he will get the first item. Have him place the item inside his blanket, then roll to the opposite side to retrieve another item. He will continue the process until he has retrieved all of the pieces of clothing, and the sushi roll is complete!

The sushi roll activity can be adjusted to fit your other routines. For example, after playtime, use the sushi roll activity to clean up the toys. This activity is a fun way to provide vestibular input as well as proprioceptive input.

HILLS AND VALLEYS

This is a fun vestibular and proprioceptive activity that can involve just your child or all of the members of the family. It is especially great to help get your child to move toward the door when it is time to go.

For a solo activity, have your child place her hands on the floor in a downward facing dog yoga pose. In this position, she is a "hill." You will have her hold this position until you shout out "valley." The "valley" position is a commando crawl. She will move across the floor until you shout out "hill"! You will continue this process until she reaches the destination.

For a group activity, the other participant will be a "hill" over the child while your child is a "valley." If performed with a sibling, have them alternate between "hills and valleys" over and under each other.

DOWNWARD FACING DOG POSE

SQUEAKY CLEAN CHECKLIST AND SONG

The purpose of this visual reminder activity is to make sure children get themselves into a habit of getting a bath, brushing their teeth, going to the bathroom, and putting on their pajamas before they go to sleep.

DIRECTIONS

All that is needed is the Squeaky Clean Checklist (see below). You may want to laminate the paper and utilize a dry erase marker. Provide your child with the checklist and have her mark off each item as it is completed. Hopefully, the task will become a habit; for example, you won't have to remind her to brush her teeth before bed. For added fun, you may also use a picture of your child in place of the image. You can also sing the Squeaky Clean song to help your child prepare for bedtime.

SQUEAKY CLEAN SONG

(to the tune of *Mary Had a Little Lamb*)

This is how I take a bath,
Take a bath,
Take a bath,
This is how I take a bath, and
Wash away the dirt.

Look at me in my pjs,
My pjs,
My pjs,
Look at me in my pjs,
I'm getting close to bedtime.

This is how I brush my teeth,
brush my teeth,
brush my teeth ,
This is how I brush my teeth, and
Wash away the cookies *(insert a fun food).*

This is how I say goodnight,
Say good night,
Say good night,
This is how I say goodnight,
Before I go to sleep.

About the Authors

Rondalyn V. Whitney, Ph.D., OTR/L, is an assistant professor and Interim Director of the Doctoral Program in the Occupational Therapy Department at the University of the Sciences in Philadelphia. Dr. Whitney focuses her writings on the barriers to optimal quality of life for families living with a child with a disability, sensory processing, and resulting social deficits in social participation. She is the author of the book *Nonverbal Learning Disorder: Understanding and Coping with NLD and Asperger's—What Parents and Teachers Need to Know*. Her new book *Writer's Toolkit* is geared toward teaching graduate students and professionals how to write successfully. She is nationally respected as a dynamic speaker on ASD and related topics such as sensory processing disorders and social skills. She is well known for her scholarship related to the use of narrative as a therapeutic modality and the use of technology and telehealth to reduce barriers of access to quality care and quality of life for families raising a child with a disability. Dr. Whitney's research interests are varied, including family quality of life, health related quality of life, toxic stress, emotional disclosure through personal narrative, and using innovative games and technology to overcome barriers to optimal care. Dr. Whitney is the former Clinical Director and founder of and innovator for the groundbreaking social skills camps and pediatric mental health intervention programs at *The Lighthouse Project* in San Jose, CA. She is a recognized leader in the occupational therapy profession. She lives in Maryland with her husband and two sons and has gained her knowledge through her journey both from raising two uniquely sensational children as well as from her professional experience.

Varleisha D. Gibbs, OTD, OTR/L, began her career after receiving her baccalaureate degree in psychology from the University of Delaware. She continued her studies in the field of occupational therapy. Dr. Gibbs received her professional degrees from Columbia University and Thomas Jefferson University. She has specific interest in children with autism spectrum disorders and sensory processing disorders and in cultural competency in treatment interventions.

In 2003, Dr. Gibbs founded Universal Progressive Therapy, Inc. located in New Jersey. The company was established with the focus of providing interdisciplinary and quality therapeutic services to families. As founding president of the company, she has had several opportunities to provide education, treatment, and study in the areas of sensory integration, autism spectrum disorders, as well as family-centered care. Dr. Gibbs has a doctoral degree in occupational therapy. She focused her doctoral studies on family-centered care, autism spectrum disorders, and the use of telerehabilitation. This innovative topic led to the publication of "Family-Centered Occupational Therapy and Telerehabilitation for Children With Autism Spectrum Disorders," found in the journal *Occupational Therapy in Healthcare.*

Dr. Gibbs has lectured and provided training on sensory processing strategies and self-regulation throughout the country. She is a full-time assistant professor in the Department of Occupational Therapy at the University of the Sciences in Philadelphia, PA. Her passions are to provide individuals with the tools that assist both the individual and the family system. Her most important occupational roles are being a wife to her husband and mother to her beautiful daughter and son.